how to **talk** to your **child** about **sex**

Also by the Authors

Lifebalance
Teaching Your Children Values
3 Steps to a Strong Family
I Didn't Plan to Be a Witch
The Awakening (a novel)
What Manner of Man
Teaching Your Children Responsibility
Teaching Your Children Sensitivity
Teaching Your Children Joy
Don't Just Do Something, Sit There
The Wrappings and the Gifts
Children's Stories to Teach Joy
Stewardship of the Heart
Spiritual Serendipity
Alexander's Amazing Adventures: Values for Children

- If you have difficulty finding any of these titles in bookstores, call (801) 581-0112 to order direct.

Linda AND Richard Eyre

how to
talk
to your
child
about
sex

it's best to start early, but it's never
too late—a step-by-step guide for
every age

Golden Books
New York

Golden Books®

888 Seventh Avenue
New York, NY 10106

Copyright © 1998 by Linda and Richard Eyre
All rights reserved, including the right of reproduction
in whole or in part in any form.
Golden Books® and colophon
are trademarks of Golden Books Publishing Co., Inc.

Designed by Stanley S. Drate/Folio Graphics Co., Inc.

Manufactured in the United States of America

10 9 8 7 6 5 4 3 2 1

Library of Congress Cataloging-in-Publication Data

Eyre, Linda.
    How to talk to your child about sex : it's best to start early,
  but it's never too late : a step-by-step guide for every age / Linda
  and Richard Eyre.
        p.   cm.
    ISBN 0-307-44072-9 (alk. paper)
    1. Sex instruction.   2. Sexual ethics.   I. Eyre, Richard M.
  II. Title.
  HQ57.E94   1998
  613.9′071—dc21   98-7581
                                                                CIP

*Special thanks to the two people
writers can't exist without—
an agent and an editor.
We're fortunate to have the best of both:
Jan Miller and Bob Asahina.*

"American kids are in the midst of their own sexual revolution, one leaving many parents feeling confused and virtually powerless."

—*Time,* June 15, 1998

Contents

Preface

When our book *Teaching Your Children Values* jumped to the number one spot on *The New York Times* best-seller list in 1993, we realized just how profoundly concerned parents are about the values their children are growing up with. And ever since then—as chapter 6 of that book, the chapter on sexual values, continued to produce the most interest, the most response, the most letters, and the most gratitude from readers—we have grown to believe that the subject of sex and the whole issue of teaching sexual responsibility and restraint may be the single greatest challenge that parents face today.

Today, as front page headlines prompt questions from our children—questions we may not be ready for, with answers our kids may not be ready for—the challenge is intensified. And what we need is not a set of simplified or "quick fix" answers. We need an offense rather than a defense, an integrated approach that helps children deal not only with the headlines, but with the big choices coming up in their own lives.

Our discussions with parents around the world, ranging from individual one-on-one conversations to question-and-answer sessions in large lecture halls, have convinced us that parents want and need practical, usable help. They want to know how to talk to their kids about sex in a positive, pragmatic way, and they want reassurance that their voice and their influence can outweigh that of the media and the peer group.

That's what we've tried to provide in this book. The bulk of it is actual "model dialogues" or sample discussions to use with your child concerning various aspects of sex and human intimacy, with the centerpiece being the "big talk" that we suggest for age eight. This pivotal discussion at eight is preceded by preparatory dialogues and followed by discussions designed to continue all through adolescence, each adaptable to your situation, your personality, and the age of your child.

The Mechanics and the Morality

The difficulty in writing a book about talking to our children about sex is that attitudes and opinions vary so widely about what is appropriate, right, and best in terms of sexual standards for both adults and children. Here is the approach we have taken and the reason for it:

In the dialogues and discussions we have constructed for this book, we have attempted to do two separate but connected things: First, give a clear model for explaining the mechanics and the facts to kids, and, second, extend most of the dialogues to include how beautiful and awesome sex can be when it happens in a committed, loyal, exclusive-love relationship. Whether you interpret that situation as marriage or as some other form of commitment is up to you. And if you choose to talk to your child only about the physical facts and mechanics of sex, you can leave out the second element of each dialogue altogether.

With this individual flexibility in mind, we decided that, if we do err, it should be on the conservative or protective side. After all, it's easier for a parent to leave out part of a dialogue than to add something in. Therefore, we've tried to give enough of the second element to satisfy the most protective parent so that *each* parent can find and use what he or she needs. And it is remarkable how conservative most parents are when it comes to their hopes and desires for their kids. A growing number hope for abstinence until marriage even if that wasn't the case in their own lives. Short of that, most parents at least want the kind of restraint that provides safety and deferment until real commitment and maturity.

So . . . don't thumb through the book and conclude that it is too conservative (or too liberal or too far right or too far left or too spiritual or too secular). *It is what you want it to be.* The dialogues are adaptable to your beliefs.

And allow for the possibility that your own beliefs and convictions about what is right and what is best for your child (and for yourself) might change as you read and contemplate, and particularly as you talk with your child. This book is written to give you options and to give you tools because *you* have the power, more than any other person on the planet, to know what is best for your child. The purpose of this book is to help you discover what that is and to succeed in teaching it.

Themes

Certain themes weave themselves throughout this book. The first two represent *opposite* approaches to most of what has been written about kids and sex over the last decade. What we read on the subject usually centers on *bigness* and *fear*. Bigness concerns the size of the problem, the huge scope, vast expense, and widespread risk of adolescent sex and teen pregnancy, and the need for broad government, legal, or educational solutions. The fear centers on the danger of promiscuity. It includes attempts to make kids aware enough (and scared enough) of the risks involved that they become more sexually responsible.

This book takes the opposite approaches of *smallness* and *love*.

Smallness: For parents, the concern is intimate and close to home—one child, their child, making good decisions and maximizing his or her chance for real love and lasting happiness. This book focuses on the interchange between individual parents and individual children. Words like "personal," "intimate," and "individual" are used frequently to remind us of this perspective.

Love: The best (and most effective) reason for sexual restraint and responsibility is that it increases one's chances for a successful and lasting long-term commitment and for a safe and happy family. A child with this goal, this hope, this vision will make better decisions in every area of his or her life. The adjectives "beautiful" and "awesome" are used repeatedly to symbolize this positive approach. The single greatest protection for kids (and the strongest motivation for avoiding early, dangerous sex) is to grow up thinking of sex as a wonderful, spectacular miracle that not only makes babies but also can bind couples and families together in a loyal, happy way. The words "beautiful and awesome" will come to represent this to your child.

We've taken these approaches because we feel that changing the micro is what changes the macro, and what we want to happen is stronger motivation than what we don't want to happen. We believe that love is the only force stronger than fear and that each strengthened family makes the world a slightly better and more beautiful place.

Besides the orientation to personal smallness and to positive love, there are five other recurrent themes in this book:

Preemptive Information: No realistic parent believes he or she can be the only source of sexual information to a child. The media, the peer group, and the school will all play large (and mixed) roles. But parents with the right message and the right timing can preempt negative and harmful information. They can also create a positive frame of reference and an effective filter through which kids can interpret and internalize what is useful and helpful to them, and screen out or set aside what is harmful or dangerous.

Family: The hope (and the goal) of all parents is to maximize the happiness and well-being of their children and help those children to one day have happy families of their own. Sex is always approached in this book as a matter of family.

The ultimate danger of the misuse of sex is the destruction of family, and the best use of sex is to strengthen the family.

Correct Principles: The most important principles that parents can convey to their children are pointedly and practically taught as families talk about sex. Open communication, delayed gratification, and the effective implementation of goals and plans are only a few of the principles that parents can teach along with and as part of a positive approach to marriage and sex.

Realism: Some fault anything other than giving in to casual, experimental sex as "unrealistic." But the best definition of "realistic" is being aware of what is really going on and acting accordingly.

Here are two candid assessments by leading writers of what is going on: Mary Pipher writes in her best-seller *The Shelter of Each Other:*

> [Our world] floods children with sexual stimulation. In magazine ads, seminude teens lock in an embrace to sell underpants or jeans. On a talk show, a man describes his sexual interest in feet. On the radio a filmmaker describes his work: "Making a movie is like simultaneously getting a blow job and getting hit on the head with a hammer." Video games often feature scantily clad, sexualized women. Home computers connect pedophiles with children learning to type. Children have scant protection from sexual messages that twenty years ago would have been taboo for grown-ups.

Leonard Pitt wrote in a Knight Ridder/Tribune News Service article on March 19, 1997:

> The world we have made is harshly different [from] the one we once knew. This culture didn't develop from that one, it mutated. These are rawer, cruder, colder times, and sexual promiscuity has become a knife's edge of danger that would have stunned us. Sex has flooded our children.

In this setting, in this reality, there is only one realistic course to take: to do all we can to protect our children and prevent them from getting into the current naive and dangerous promiscuity that can harm them in so many ways.

A Focus on the Personal: Because of the personal nature of the subject matter, we have tried to write this book in a very personal way. Each part of the book ends in a personal interlude: personal tips for parents, a personal experience about losing a major publisher over our insistence on the importance of teaching sexual values, responses and reactions from our own children; a fable or bedtime story that is one of our family favorites, a recollection of a pivotal dinner conversation, and a conversation with old friends who had given up on the idea of sexual restraint for their kids—for all the wrong reasons.

Our challenge to you is to read the book as personally as it is written. Apply it to your own children and to your own life.

Aha!s and Yeah, Buts

We think every serious reader of this book will experience a couple of recurring reactions. One will be the aha!s . . . little feelings of illumination or insight: "Aha! I understand that, and I think it's right." The other will be the yeah, buts . . . little excuses or exceptions that may follow the aha!s: "Yeah, but that won't work for me and my kids."

Our first challenge to you is to *accept* the aha!'s. When something feels right for your child, let that idea or concept in, let it take root, and let it "win out" over what you've been doing or what is easier or what everyone else is doing—even over what you think is realistic. Our second challenge is to push aside the yeah, buts. The approaches and dialogues suggested in this book are not easy for anyone, and teaching both the facts and the restraint of sexual responsibility is a challenge for every parent. It will be a natural impulse to find reasons that it won't work in your particular situation, why you can't do it, why your child won't listen. But none of these reasons will help your child. So fight through them and do your best. Progress may be slow, but with a persevering, determined attitude, you *will* make a difference.

One of the main yeah, buts may be, "Yeah, but my family is not like the Eyres. They just sound too perfect." Let us put your mind at ease on that point. When we hear something like that, our reaction is a mixture of laughter and panic. We think, "If you only knew . . ." but we also fear that people will not realize the one single fact that qualifies us to write books for other parents: We are fellow strugglers! Our perspectives come from real experiences with lots of very normal (and often very difficult) kids. We don't write about every problem we've had—who wants a ten-volume book?—but the problems and challenges we've faced and struggled with have given us the courage to write.

Your circumstances and situations as a parent are completely unique, as are ours, but this book is not about circumstances and situations. It's about the challenge of teaching our kids to be sexually responsible and, ultimately, sexually happy. And that challenge is essentially the same for all of us. May we meet it!

Linda and Richard Eyre

Introduction

What Parents Face Today

Talking to kids about sex has never been easy. And today it's more complicated than ever and more critical than ever. Our children are exposed (in every sense of that word) to more sex from more sources than ever before.

Before getting to the dialogues and discussions designed to increase the influence you have on your child's sexual destiny, it's important to look more closely at the problem in order to understand what we're up against and to come to believe that we can meet the challenge.

The Problem

The difficulty and embarrassment of talking to our kids about sex has almost become a cultural cliché: the nervous, red-faced parent groping for the right words to use with a tittering young son or daughter who finally says, "Oh, don't worry, Mom [or Dad]. I already know all about sex."

And it's not just a matter of being "too late" with this kind of discussion. True, discussions between parents and children about sexual topics are happening more and more often because of their predominance in the media. Yet a surprising number of parents never have "the talk" with their kids, let alone an ongoing, open communication about the physical, emotional, and spiritual aspects of sex.

Parents who do talk to their kids about sex often do so in a context of fear, danger, and warning, which prompts rebellion and experimentation in some kids and negative, joy-robbing inhibition in others.

The problem, of course, runs much deeper than our own embarrassment or procrastination, and deeper than our kids' rebellion or inhibition. Our parental inaction and ineffectiveness in this regard bring about sexual attitudes, mores, and behavior that lead to or contribute to a whole host of related problems.

On the macro or societal level, irresponsible sexual activity is a problem of such huge dimensions that it can scarcely be grasped or measured. The direct economic costs of teen pregnancy are enormous; the indirect costs of the associated welfare, judicial, and correctional needs are staggering; and the emotional costs are unmeasurable.

On the micro or family and individual level, casual and promiscuous sexual activity and destructive and negative sexual attitudes pull families apart; cause wrenching, emotionally scarring decisions about abortion; short-circuit education and careers; and spread physical and emotional illness.

Parents may understand some or all of this, but they may feel inadequate or incapable of advising their children effectively. It's easy to feel overwhelmed by the insidious messages offered by the media and the peer group: "Everyone does it—and without consequences." But studies and surveys show that parents who are committed, who make the effort, can have much more influence over their children than any other factor or force.

The Solution

The solution will never be legislated, written into a school curriculum, or packaged in a simple video or an interactive CD-ROM. The solution must be in homes and families, and must come from parents.

This book lays out a simple series of discussions for parents to have with their young children about sex, safety, commitment, and marriage. The discussions are positive and promote emotional bonding between parent and child. Properly approached, they will not be awkward or uncomfortable for either parent or child.

Parents will be able to overcome embarrassment and gain confidence when using these discussions because they are simple and clear, and have been developed and refined through use with a wide variety of children.

The solution, in other words, lies in communication. This is, above all else, a book about parents communicating with their children. While most of the discussions center on sex and human intimacy, topics such as drinking and drugs, savings and economics, decision-making skills, and even historical and statistical perspectives are also included. Remember this: A parent and child who can communicate honestly and openly about the most intimate subject of sex will find it easy to communicate about other subjects.

Parents who commit themselves to ongoing, open communication, who think it through and decide what they truly believe is best regarding their children and sex—what is healthiest and happiest for them physically, mentally, emotionally, socially, and spiritually—and who take the time and find the right tools to help their children come to the same conclusions are parents who will not only have the solutions but will *be* the solutions.

The Results and the Promise

Forgive some parental pride here, but we're making the beginning of a point about *results*. As we write this book, the oldest of our nine children is twenty-six and has just finished her graduate degree at Harvard. Our next daughter is a new mom and works with her husband at the Points of Light Foundation in Washington, D.C. Our youngest is eleven and going into sixth grade. Among the other six, four are at college or studying abroad, and two are in high school, living at home. They are all spirited, unique, independent individuals. We've had the "age eight discussion" (and the prediscussions and follow-up discussions this book suggests) nine different times. And they have worked! Each of our nine children has a positive, wholesome attitude toward sex, and each has avoided teen or preteen sexual encounters and the physical and emotional dangers that come with them. All nine want the security and commitment of fidelity within their marriages.

And it's not just us! We head a parents' cooperative organization called SJS HOMEBASE with a membership of over one hundred thousand parents across the country and around the world. People who have used these and similar methods have had resounding success teaching their children about sex and keeping them safe from premature experimentation.

And it's not just these SJS HOMEBASE parents who have managed to be a stronger influence on their children than the media or the peer group in matters of sex and intimacy.

The evidence is overwhelming that any parent who puts his or her mind to it, and who has the confidence of the right approach and the right tools, can teach a child to view sex positively and responsibly; that a parent can protect his or her child from the devastating physical and emotional dangers of experimental, casual, or promiscuous sexual activity and enhance the child's chance for a stable, happy, committed marriage and family.

The Format

This book is made up of five sections of dialogues and discussions: Preliminary "As Needed" Talks with Three- to Eight-Year-Olds, The Age Eight "Big Talk," Follow-Up Talks with Eight- to Thirteen-Year-Olds, Behavior Discussions with Eleven- to Sixteen-Year-Olds, Discussions of Perspective and Personal Standards with Fifteen- to Nineteen-Year-Olds. The age overlaps allow for different physical and emotional maturity levels and for different situations in various communities.

These five age-specific discussion sections are interspersed with our comments to parents and our personal experiences and those of our children. These personal interludes appear at the end of each dialogue and discussion section.

Remember that the five sections and age designations are not different ways to have the same talk with kids of different ages. Rather, they are a sequence or series of small, related discussions that start with subjects suitable for children as young as three and progress to those aimed at kids as old as eighteen or nineteen. The suggested ages are the *ideal* timetable for the discussions, and there are clear advantages to starting with very young children and progressing through the age categories as they are presented. If you start later with a child, there are suggestions for adapting the discussions that might ideally have come earlier. See particularly the discussion sections titled "Older Than Twelve" and "Starting Over."

Once you have completed The Age Eight "Big Talk," the final three sections are separated not only by age but by the type and tone of their subject matter. The eight-to-thirteen section centers on discussions of basic facts about puberty, maturation, and a wide range of sex-related subjects. The eleven-to-sixteen section deals principally with behavior and with the dangers of adolescence. And the fifteen-to-nineteen section is designed to help high school–age kids form clear-headed perspectives and personal standards. The sequence and topical progression of these three sections can be summarized as follows:

AGE	TOPICS	PARENTS' ROLE	GOAL
8–13	Basics	Teacher	Preemptive—hearing about things from you first
11–16	Behavior	Manager	Retard social growth
15–19	Beliefs	Consultant	To do the right things for the right reasons

Questions and Answers

We conclude most of the lectures and seminars we give to parents with a question-and-answer session. The following are the most common questions parents have and some of the answers we offer.

Question: Why is it so hard to talk to your own kids about sex (so hard that a shocking number of parents never do it)?

Answer: There are three reasons: the embarrassment we recall about the subject and our own conscious and subconscious inhibitions, our lack of a plan or an agenda or a clear idea of what we ought to say and how we ought to say it, and our own ambiguity about what we ourselves believe about sex and what we want our children to believe.

Question: Even with help—proven methods, dialogues, and so forth—can a parent compete with media and peers as a major influence in how kids think about sex?

Answer: Yes! A parent who starts early and knows what he or she is doing can be the dominant influence, superseding and overwhelming all other voices.

Question: Does talking with my child about sex have to be uncomfortable and embarrassing for both of us?

Answer: No! Quite the contrary. If you do it at the right time and in the right way, it can be enjoyable and natural—and can build a powerful and deep emotional bond between you and your child that facilitates other kinds of communication and trust.

Question: Is it harder for a single parent to talk to kids about sex?

Answer: Yes and no. It may be harder in the sense that you're on your own, without a spouse to support you or to do part of the discussing or to help sort out how to approach it, but the objective and the principles are the same. In a way it is easier because you're the only one doing it. You have control and consistency in what you say and in how and when you say it. A lot of single parents, because they're on their own, take their responsibility more seriously and actually do a better job. (Although the plural, *parents,* is often used in this book, be assured that everything herein is equally applicable and equally intended for single parents.)

Question: What is the most important thing when talking to kids about sex?

Answer: The single most important thing is to make it a positive, exciting, joyful subject and to link the subject to marriage and family and to love and commitment in a clear and positive way.

Question: Is eight really the best age for the "big talk"? Some would say it's too early, some would say too late.

Answer: It is important to have your main discussion (and your pre- and follow-up discussions) early enough that they form your child's initial attitudes toward sex and serve as a deflector of all the "silliness," "dirtiness," and nonsense that children hear from friends, peers, and media. But having it too early raises issues that kids aren't ready for.

Question: Is the objective here to protect my child, to make her aware of the physical and emotional dangers of sex?

Answer: Yes and no. We do need to protect our children, but it is an awareness of the beautiful power and positive commitment in the right kind of sex that gives children the best motivation and capacity to avoid what could hurt them and others.

Question: As a parent, is it unusual for me to hope my child approaches sex more carefully and more conservatively than I did? Am I a hypocrite if I try to teach my child to abstain in ways I did not?

Answer: It is very common for parents to wish their children would wait for real commitment (because of physical safety, emotional safety, moral beliefs, hopes of a better marriage—and a host of other reasons). Most parents' views are surprisingly conservative when it comes to what they wish for and think is best for their children. And it is not hypocritical to teach something you have not always lived, especially if you truly feel it is what is best for today. Good parenting means wanting something better for one's children!

Question: But is it realistic to hope for (and work for) less sexual activity before commitment and marriage?

Answer: The facts indicate that it is. More and more respected thinkers are concluding that this form of "delayed gratification" is smarter as well as safer. And things are changing: Kids in age groups who didn't want to admit they were virgins five years ago now feel pride in the fact. But these are individual decisions, and the overwhelming reality is that parents need to decide what course is best for their children and then take concrete, positive steps to improve their children's chances of taking that course.

Question: But can I decide what is best for my child, or does he have the right to grow up and decide for himself?

Answer: Let us repeat the metaphor from our book *Teaching Your Children Values:* "Expecting a young child to discover what is right for him is like putting him in a small boat, in the current, without a paddle, heading for Niagara Falls." Of course a child will eventually decide for himself, but *not* to teach him what our experience (and our heart) tells us is best is the most serious form of parental abdication of responsibility.

Question: But what if I'm not sure what is best?

Answer: One of the most demanding (and most beneficial) parts of parenting is sorting out what we believe, so we can teach those beliefs with honesty to our children. No one can do that for you, but this book may help.

Question: How much does the media's portrayal of sex influence our children? Does casual, irresponsible, or indifferent sex in the media harm us as much as casual, irresponsible, or indifferent violence in media?

Answer: Media sex is actually a bigger danger than media violence. A tiny percentage of kids copy or reenact the violence they see, but countless thousands imitate the irresponsible, uncommitted, casual sex that they see nearly every time they turn on the TV or go to a movie. Perhaps if kids carried Uzi machine guns around with them, they would imitate more of the violence they see. They do carry their sexuality around with them, so the potential for imitation is truly frightening. The directly related societal costs of teen pregnancy, abortion, disease, and depression that result make teenage sexual activity the biggest social problem facing America today and make irresponsible media sex a huge culprit.

Question: What if my child is already sexually active?

Answer: *Don't give up!* It's never too late to make the subject of sex more open and more positive between you and your child. *Don't give in!* If you believe that waiting for real love and commitment is best, is *right*, then don't give in to the status quo. There is a whole movement in this country about "regaining virginity," about deciding to wait for marriage. *Don't give out!* Don't get too tired to try. Don't ever abdicate this part of your parental responsibility. Adapt the discussions suggested in this book. Make particular use of the section entitled "Starting Over." Stay positive. Let the child know that you love him unconditionally but are concerned about the things he is doing. Be specific. Help him sort it out.

Summary Questions

The simplest, shortest questions provide the best overview:

Q. Who?   **A.** You! You as the parent must take the lead and set the tone for how your child will think about sex. Your influence can supersede that of the media, the peer group, and the school.

Q. What?   **A.** Not only the physiological "facts of life" but the emotional and spiritual importance of committed sexual love. You can teach it *all* to your child.

Q. What?   (What if you're not too confident in your own knowledge of the subject?)
                   A. Then you've bought the right book!

Q. Where?   **A.** In your home and family. That is the place for the commitment and intimacy of sex, and for discussions about it.

Q. When?   **A.** Eight-year-old children (some are ready as early as seven) are the most open, natural, curious, positive, impressionable, and appreciative—and the least cynical or embarrassed. This is the best time for the big talk, but remember that the goal is not one discussion but an ongoing openness and dialogue with your child that starts as early as age three and continues throughout life!

Q. How?   **A.** This is the question that most of this book is devoted to: how to bring it up, how to make it positive and thorough, how to follow up, how to create and maintain trust and honesty, how to draw closer than ever before on topics of intimacy, marriage, and family.

Q. Why?   **A.** Beyond the obvious reasons of protection, safety, and marital happiness, this is an area that, when handled well, can do two profoundly important things for families:

1. *Keep communication open.* Parents and children who are successful in communicating about this most intimate subject find that the barriers come down on other subjects.

2. *Foster delayed gratification.* Children who learn the principle of "waiting" and "saving" regarding sex are in a better position to avoid the search for instant gratification that is so rampant in our society and so economically and emotionally destructive.

PERSONAL TIPS FOR PARENTS

Timing, Content, and Techniques—the When, the What, and the How

Before outlining dialogues and discussions for your adaptation and use with your children, we would like to make a few personal comments and suggestions that may help. Remember that each of our children and each of yours is unique and that every family is unique. Everything we present here can be modified and tailored to fit what you know about your child's needs and characteristics. Trust your own instincts and insights, and enjoy your efforts to communicate with your child about a subject so intimate and so beautiful that it can "open the way" for better communication about all subjects!

Timing

The timing is a matter of balance—not telling children too much, too early, before they're interested or ready to understand, but not waiting until they know too much from negative, incomplete, wrong sources. We feel that the peak of a child's readiness is at age eight, when he or she is very verbal and conceptual and is flattered by responsibility and by being treated as a "grown up." This age is like a marvelous window. Kids are old enough to understand but not old enough to be cynical. They are old enough to have real interest and fascination but not old enough to be embarrassed or closed off or to have a lot of preconceptions. Before the big talk, you should hold some preliminary discussions to prepare the way. And after the big talk there are a number of related subjects that need to be discussed in more detail. Then, as your child enters and experiences adolescence, the focus shifts from facts to behavior, from *knowing* what he should to *doing* what he should, and to acting with restraint and responsibility.

(If your child is between eight and twelve, the "big talk" suggested here is still workable and appropriate but will have to be modified so it doesn't sound as if you're "talking down" to your child and to allow for a child who knows more and probably has more questions.)

Dialogues and Discussions

Over the years, in our lectures and seminars for parents on talking with their children about sex, we've tried a number of approaches. We've been theoretical: "Here's why it's important, and here are the principles you should follow." We've suggested they sit down with their children and ask them what questions they have. We've tried giving parents sequences or outlines of what to say. But the most useful and most appreciated approach appears to be actual dialogues. For most parents this makes the task approachable, doable, practical, real. They may not follow the dialogues exactly (and the kids definitely won't always give the expected or hoped-for answers), but a real dialogue is a track to run on. It ensures that each critical point is covered, and it gives a parent the confidence of knowing that he is not alone and is not trying something new. These dialogues have been tested and proven, tried and adjusted—and they work!

Besides, the title of this book is *How to Talk to Your Child About Sex.* "How" implies something concrete, not theoretical, so we think actual sample dialogues are the best way to fulfill the promise of the book's title.

A sample or model dialogue is provided not only for the age eight big talk but for many of the suggested "before" (preparation) talks and "after" (follow-up) talks. We've chosen an arbitrary child's name to use in each dialogue, and whether it is a boy's or girl's name, be assured that the dialogues work equally well for children of both genders, although sometimes a slight—and obvious—modification may be needed. For the later talks with adolescent children, we've provided fewer sample dialogues and more "discussion points" and thought-prompting essays that can be read and then discussed.

With both the dialogues and the discussions, feel free to use this book openly with your child. It's okay to read directly from the book if that is more comfortable than using your own words. And it's okay to let your child read whatever parts of this book he wants to read, although his reading should never replace your discussions with him.

Create a tone of openness about the whole subject of sex and about this book. If you choose to read parts of the dialogues or discussions, introduce the book to your child: "I've found a book that lots of parents and kids use to help them talk about and understand sex. Sometimes when we're talking about sex I'll read parts of it to you or ask you questions from it."

Boldness

As you read through the dialogues and discussions that follow, your reaction may be "I can't just launch into that with my child" or "She won't listen to me on that" or "That's going to be awkward" or "I don't think we're ready for something quite that direct."

Often we're too timid as parents, and our timidity lessens our authority and effectiveness because kids don't respect us as much or listen to us as carefully. Remind yourself that you are the parent and have stewardship and responsibility for your child. You know far more about most things than he does. You love him. You want him to make good decisions, especially when it comes to tough choices.

The discussions that follow are, among other things, a way for you to improve on your boldness. The end result of a committed, sustained effort to have these discussions will be more respect from your child and far deeper communication on this and other subjects. If you've been a bit timid in the past, your first efforts may be rebuffed with silence or with "I don't want to talk about it." But persist. Act with authority. Tell your child that your reason is love—that you love him so much, you will do all you can to help him know what he needs to know to make good choices and be happy.

Be bold, be persistent, be loving. Make these discussions a priority. It will pay off.

Getting the Right Responses

In the dialogues, the child's response, in parentheses, follows the parent's question. Often it will simply say "Response" because the dialogue proceeds irrespective of what the child says. When a particular kind of answer is called for, a sample response is printed. These samples are common responses that came from real kids as the dialogues were being developed and tested. Obviously, your child will not say exactly the same things, but you will be able to lead your child to similar answers by giving clues or shorter "subquestions."

For example, when you ask, "How do you show someone you love her?" and your child just shrugs, ask a subquestion such as, "Well, how do I show that I love you?" or "How do you show Grandma you love her?" until you get some variation of the desired response: "Tell them, do nice things for them, give them a kiss or a hug."

Or when you ask, "What kind of people would be the best parents?" your child may say, "I don't know." You can say, "Well, would love be important?" Your child will say yes. You say, "Would being able to take good care of a child be important?" Your child says yes. You say, "So to be a good mom or dad, you'd have to be old enough to . . . what?" "Love a baby and take care of it" is the response. Where it is likely kids will need prompting, the text will say "(help and clues)" in the sample response.

Following Their Lead and Their Attention Span

Don't become so committed to the printed dialogues that you miss opportunities to pick up on questions or on detours your child might lead you on. Remember that *listening* and *awareness* will often provide you with a natural way to get into a particular subject. And even while having a particular discussion or dialogue, a question or comment might lead you to another one.

It's a good idea to read all the dialogues once before you use any of them in order to know enough about what they say and where they are in the book so you can shift from one to another as the opportunity presents itself.

But don't wait for questions in every case. Remember the "preemptive" objective and follow your own instincts to know the right time.

Also respect your child's attention span. Generally, a "dialogue" approach will lengthen it, while a "lecture" shortens it. Still, when you feel interest or attention waning, wrap up and save the rest for another day.

Staying Positive and Building Confidence

The best way to keep a discussion going, to keep the interest and energy level high, and to make it a positive experience for your child is to give abundant praise for every good or well-intended answer.

The dialogues frequently use words like "exactly" and "good answer." Expand these according to what your child says: "It just amazes me how thoughtful you are about these things" or "I enjoy talking to you about this; it's like talking to another adult" or "What a good answer! I think you're really getting this!"

1

Preliminary "As Needed" Talks with Three- to Eight-Year-Olds

This section outlines discussions to have with preschool and early elementary age children in preparation for the "big talk." The suggested dialogues deal with the physical body, awe and wonder in nature and the physical world, family commitment, loyalty and love, and "modesty" based on respect. Ideas and instruction are given on how to answer younger children's simple questions without going beyond the questions.

Answering Questions Without
Going Beyond Them

A mother told us a funny (but point-making) story. Her five-year-old son came up to her one evening at home and said, "Mom, where did I come from?" She thought of trying to detour or escape the question somehow, but there was no ready excuse. The two of them were alone at home that night, and she figured that if her son was asking, she'd better summon up her courage and tell him.

They sat down in the living room, and the mother launched into it, not too smoothly and feeling a little embarrassed, but giving it her best shot. The little boy's eyes got wider and wider as he listened without a word, just nodding his head slightly whenever his mother said, "Do you understand that?" and shaking his head slowly whenever she said, "Did you know that?" When she was finished, she said, "Does that answer your question?"

The little fellow squirmed around and said, "Well . . . I just meant . . . you know . . . where did we come from? Like before we moved here last year. I forgot the name of our other town."

While usually not as dramatically as in this story, it is easy to tell very young children too much. The best policy, until they are seven or eight, is just to respond to their questions, their *real* questions, with simple answers, always deferring detail to later and using the interchange as a way to build a positive anticipation for when they turn eight.

So if a five-year-old says, "Where do babies come from?" say, "Sometimes when a mommy and daddy love each other, it helps make a baby." If he says, "But *how?*" say, "It's like a miracle, a wonderful, unbelievable magic. When you're eight, we'll tell you about it."

If your belief or faith supports it, an even better answer might be "Babies are a gift from our Heavenly Father. He puts them into our families." If there is a persisting "But how?" say, "Well, it happens in a really wonderful, awesome way, and when you turn eight, we'll tell you about it."

Then change the subject unless you detect that the child is troubled or worried or has heard something that is causing him to persist. If this is the case, probe. Find out what he has heard or what has happened. If it's just a word or term he's heard that he doesn't understand, give your best explanation and say, "That's one thing we'll talk about when you're eight." If he has heard a joke or an off-color story about sex, you may want to say, "Some people joke around or say weird things about stuff they don't understand. But don't worry, we'll tell you all about it when you're eight. And believe me, it is wonderful and really cool!"

Appreciation for Bodies

A healthy attitude about sex starts with how a child feels about his own body. At a very young age children become aware of their bodies and what they can do. In fact, studies have shown that over 80 percent of what we learn about our physical bodies is learned in the first eighteen months of life. We see this when watching our four-month-old grandchild realize that the thing attached to the end of his arm can be used to move things that are in front of him and that he can see a different view by pushing off with one leg and one arm while balancing with the other two appendages to make the magnificent effort to turn his whole body over! Babies learn more about how to manage their physical bodies in that short time than they will for the rest of their lifetime.

As children grow, they often maintain their childlike spontaneous delight in the interesting things that are happening around them, but without our help they don't fully understand the marvelous miracle that is called their body. They take for granted that they can see their mother's face and hear cars racing by as they mutilate a piece of bread while sitting in their car seat.

We've seen how older preschoolers continued to find awe and wonder in their bodies while observing thousands of kids go through our Joy Schools (a series of do-it-yourself preschool lesson plans designed for three-, four-, and five-year-olds), especially the unit called "The Joy of the Body." This preschool curriculum, based on *Teaching Your Children Joy*, is an alternative to pushy, early academic approaches. Included are hundreds of creative ways to help young children appreciate the magic of their bodies, from dancing in the leaves to classical music to taping their thumbs to the rest of their hands for a short time to help them appreciate how valuable their thumbs are. Kids revel in appreciating all that their body can do.

As children grow older, their basic attitude about their body and how it functions becomes part of their reference for how they feel about using their bodies as an adult to show love and to feel joy in a physical sexual relationship. Learning how the body can conceive and produce a child fits their framework of the joyful, miraculous nature of the body.

In dealing with young children, every available opportunity should be taken to point out how lucky we are to be able to see the beauties of the season, to hear creative and inspirational music, to taste different and unique combinations of food (a couple of our children would not call this a joy), to touch a baby's cheek or a kitten's soft fur, and especially to feel the love that we have for the others in our family. The list of things to point out and be grateful for is endless. The more a child can appreciate his own body as a preschooler, the better foundation he will have for feeling positive about the greatest of all physical miracles.

Awe and Wonder in Nature

I (Linda) think our appreciation for nature peaked during our first year of graduate school in Boston. I was working long, hard hours and coming home with just enough energy to make a dinner, prepare a lesson plan for the next day, and drop into bed beside Richard, who was working day and night on his assignments for the Harvard Business School, where he was slogging his way toward a degree. Newly married and with a brand-new baby, we were woefully poor, and the only form of recreation we could afford was to observe nature. We sat by the Charles River and watched the crews go by, stroking in unison through water so calm that it looked as if they were gliding through unset Jell-O. By October we were appreciating the intricate workings of nature that produced an incredible fairyland of autumn color. It was there that we made a pact with each other to teach our children the awe and wonder of nature and appreciation for how a loving God made things work together for our enjoyment. Through the years we made a conscious effort to point out to our children the ever-changing beauty of the natural world. We later realized that our emphasis on nature and its beauty made it easier and more natural to talk to the kids about the miracle of the functions of their bodies.

If anything, we may have gone a bit overboard with the "beauty of nature" emphasis. Sometimes we wondered if we were just a little bit crazy as we heaped giant piles of leaves together at the city park on Richard's birthday in October and stuffed them down each other's backs and threw them in the air with wild shrieks of delight. Our first son-in-law-to-be must have wondered what kind of family we were as we screeched to a stop just outside Jackson Hole, Wyoming, one summer evening, to jump out of the car and do a little jig when we saw the clouds lift to reveal what we were treating as our long-lost relatives: the Teton Mountains.

Interestingly, a letter came from our oldest daughter, Saren, yesterday as I was contemplating writing on this subject. She was our babe in arms as we started our life together in Boston. Things have now come full circle, and she is just finishing her own Harvard graduate degree. Our sixteen-year-old son, Noah, went out to visit her for a few days last week.

Excerpts from her letter about her present life and her adventures with Noah demonstrate just what effect those long-ago talks about nature are having now on this twenty-six-year-old daughter. (So you won't think she is obsessed with nature, please know that I have extracted only the parts that deal with the subject at hand.)

> *September 30: It's almost midnight and then it will be October. I'm excited. I think October is my favorite month. . . . The hecticness of starting new things that generally comes with September is over and the weather is soft and crisp and the leaves are lovely. I'm trying to get back to my poetic self to some degree because I've just been losing track of the forest for all the trees. A friend of mine shared with me a quote that has really helped me: "There is always music amongst the trees in the garden, but our hearts must be very quiet to hear." I haven't been hearing the music lately and I haven't felt like I'm in a garden at all. My heart's been feeling burdened and tromped on and stretched and certainly not quiet. I haven't been appreciating and savoring the beauty all around enough—the evening light on my favorite sycamore trees along Memorial Drive, the pink sky over the Charles as I drive home from work, the fuchsia and gold leaves boldly taking over a brazen branch here and there, the crunch of new autumn leaves underfoot, the spontaneous smile and hug of a small child.*

> *Overview of my time with Noah:*
> *Thursday—late night pickup at the airport, driving back along Storrow Drive—the Citgo sign and the lights in the river. Taking a walk on a perfect fall night along the Charles—touch of rain, crossing Weeks Bridge, looking at Peabody Terrace and walking around the Business School, talking about Mom and Dad and thinking about how things come full circle.*

Friday—we walked through the Public Gardens—the perfect flowers and still pond. We picked gingko leaves and collected fresh fallen chestnuts. Talked a lot about ambiance. Ended up at a Thai restaurant with some friends. Noah passed the time by playing with his chopsticks, sticking them up his nose or using his lips to maneuver them. He sort of reminded me of this crazy fish in the tank behind him—a big goldfish with two big funny teeth sticking out.

Saturday—borrowed bikes and went on a long bike ride—up the Charles and all over the Harvard campus— such a perfect fall day! Went on a drive out to the end of the peninsula to climb around on the rocks and watch the sky turn pink as the waves crashed against the rocks. I love the ocean. And waves crashing on rocks just fills me with joy for some reason.

Sunday—Noah was quite taken with Trinity Church— we marveled at the beauty, rich colors, golds, rusty reds, dusty blues, interesting patterns, beautiful stained glass, wonderful carvings. So good to see anything beautiful created for the glory and worship of God. Walked home after church—gorgeous day again. Talked until late at night about dating, kissing, the whole thing. Noah's so fun to talk to.

Monday—went to see the new OmniMax movie "The Living Sea" at the Science Museum—amazing. Noah LOVED it and decided to become a marine biologist. Got lost trying to find gas on the way to the airport. Beautiful colors emerging on the trees. I LOVE FALL!

Appreciation and love for the miraculous creations of the earth have everything to do with the groundwork needed to have a successful first discussion with your child on the most amazing, powerful, miraculous thing in the world—the process of bringing a new child into it. Look for the opportunity to have frequent little discussions like the following:

DIALOGUE

Wow, Tom. Come out here on the balcony and look at this amazing sunset!

Tom: I'm right in the middle of a computer game.

Guess what, Tommy! This big surprise that nature has provided outside right this very minute is more fantastic than anything you will ever see on a computer! I need a friend to enjoy it with. You're so good at noticing colors and beautiful things in nature. I want you to come and tell me what you see! That game will still be there a few minutes from now, but this sunset will happen only once. Let's go!

OR:

Hey, Jill. Do you notice anything different in our backyard?

Jill: No.

Well, the oak tree is just starting to turn slightly green and get little buds. It's gorgeous. When you go out today, see what else you can notice and tell me about it when I get home from work, okay?

Your enthusiasm and positive attitude will heighten your child's awareness. Take the opportunity to point out the beauties that you see in the colors, contrasts, shading, and textures as you experience nature with your children on walks, bike rides, campouts, and hikes. Your observations will make them think and will stimulate them to think of their pleasure as they observe nature. When your child is seven, you can turn your comments on nature into anticipation builders for the big talk, such as:

Jill, when we go out for our special talk on your eighth birthday, we're going to tell you about something that has to do with nature. But it's even more amazing than the beautiful things you always notice about the trees and rocks, plants and animals. Do you realize that everything in nature is absolutely unique? No two leaves are alike, even on the same tree. Every flower is different from any other flower. No two people are alike, either, and that's part of what we'll talk about when you're eight. Nature is truly awesome!

Family Commitments, Loyalty, and Love

There is no argument about the fact that it is easier to teach your small children about family commitment, loyalty, and love if you grew up with it in your childhood and if you feel it now with your spouse. Those who were raised with these idyllic qualities will most probably teach them to their children rather easily and naturally.

On the other hand, those who have been touched by the tragedy of a parent who had an affair or did not follow through on commitments or, hardest of all, did not show love may find it harder to teach these concepts. Yet it is often these very parents who do a more conscientious job with their own children because of their burning desire that their kids *not* experience the same thing.

Recently I (Linda) spent an evening with friends who had recently married and were attempting to blend a new family. As I asked questions of this vibrant, happy couple, I discovered that the father of the family had been an Olympic athlete in the recent past. Knowing the requirements of self-discipline, hard work, and dedication to be an Olympic athlete, I said, "Your parents must be very proud of you!"

"I don't really have much of a relationship with my parents," he said. "They are very tight-lipped about everything. If they were proud of me, they never told me about it. As a result, my family has been pretty fractured. We just don't communicate much."

I was devastated by his comment, but he went right on talking about his eight-year-old son and his wife's seven-year-old son and their delight in seeing them become "suddenly brothers." This man was obviously making a concentrated effort to provide the commitment, love, and loyalty for this new family that he had lacked in his own childhood.

What do commitment, love, and loyalty have to do with talking to your children about sex? Everything! Whether you are reading this as a loyal, committed, loving spouse and parent who was also lucky enough to grow up in a close family, or as a single parent who has had no role modeling for these qualities now or in childhood, you *can* talk to your kids about them. Whether your model is something you've experienced or something you've wished for, you can share your feelings with your children. If you have always been exposed to loyalty, love, and commitment, tell your child about it. Share some of the childhood experiences you can remember about how your parents showed their love for each other and express how much you love your spouse, their other parent. Add stories of family loyalty—cheering at your brother's games even though you were a little jealous that he got all the attention, your dad showing up at your birthday party even though it was difficult for him, the love you felt from your parents as they tucked you in bed and praised you for a job well done. Kids love to hear stories about you as a child with their grandparents as parents.

If you grew up in difficult circumstances or have been hurt by unfaithfulness or family disloyalty, tell your children a little about it and reassure them of your commitment to never let it happen in your own family. At bedtime or some other appropriate setting say something like: "I think one of the most important things in a family is to know that we love each other. I will always love you, and you will always be the most important thing in my life. No matter how hard life gets outside these walls, you need to know that our family will always be here for you. It wasn't always that way for me." Share a story of a disappointment that you may have had as a child and say now that you're grown you understand it a little better and are trying to forgive the person who made you sad. Your child will get the idea that even though you have gone through some pain because of lack of commitment, loyalty, and love in your own family, you want something much better for them. Then walk your talk!

Whether you come from a happy family you want to replicate or a problematic family you want to improve on, you can use your own experiences as a backdrop to love and reassure your child. As you do, you will be creating a substantial foundation for the talks about sex that will follow because your child will understand how important a strong, committed relationship is to you. Don't assume that your child knows you are completely committed to your family and to him as an individual. Tell him!

Children should hear these words: "I love you." "I am so proud of the way you are choosing to do the right thing even when it is hard." "Our family is our first priority." "No matter how hard and demanding things are at work, my heart is with you!" You can't say these things too often!

Modesty in Dress and Appearance

Modesty is sort of an old-fashioned word. It is not used much anymore and belongs in the same category as chastity—something straight out of a Charlotte Brontë novel. It is not even in the vocabulary of a modern preadolescent anymore, right? Certainly the part about the word not being in our preadolescent's vocabulary is true. And in our conversations with our young daughters, "What do you think about modesty?" is just not up there with, "Is your room clean?" and "Is your homework done?" Yet parents have to be concerned as their children walk out the door dressed in a way that leaves little to the imagination or with a new hole pierced somewhere in their bodies.

Once again, timing is crucial. The time to talk to your daughter about caring for her body, the implications and significance of what she wears, and treating her body with respect is not on the day she comes home with a new tattoo on her shoulder. Start with preschoolers, kindergarteners, and first graders. Having "modesty" conversations with young children can guide their thinking about what clothes they will choose and how they are going to deal with their bodies as they mature. Even if friends try and sometimes succeed in influencing your child's decisions about dress and conduct, your preliminary talks are the best anchor as your child sets goals and makes decisions concerning standards.

DIALOGUE

Hillary, I can't believe how nice you look today. You are growing up! Before you know it, you'll be a teenager. Are you looking forward to that time?

Response.

What do you think it will be like to be a teenager?

Hillary: I don't know.

What kind of a teenager do you want to be?

Hillary [help and clues]: I want to be happy, do well in school, and so forth.

If you could be just like a teenager you know right now, who would it be?

Response. [Hope that your child chooses someone with admirable personality traits. She may also choose the opposite. In either case, probe the answer. Ask what she likes about this person. If she can't think of anyone, suggest a sister or a cousin or neighbor whom you think she might admire and talk about what you both like about that person.]

There are so many exciting things about being a teenager, but there are a few dangers, too, that you should be thinking about a little bit. There are some pretty crazy teenagers in this world. Most of them are trying to make a statement about how they feel about the world. They show it in the way they dress and the way they act. Some kids just a little older than you wear things that are very strange, don't you agree?

Response.

You have been given a very special body. It does amazing things for you, and you need to take good care of it. Sometimes kids forget how important it is to use their bodies wisely and take good care of them. They see things on TV and in movies that make them think the most important thing in the world is to look beautiful or grown-up. They start thinking that a good way to get a boyfriend is to wear clothes that are short and tight and show off their bodies. They think the only way people will view them as cool is if they have great-looking bodies. Many of them think they are fat even when they aren't a bit fat, and they start doing crazy things to their bodies to make themselves look the way they think others want them to look. That's kind of sad, isn't it?

Response.

Hillary, because I love you so much, I don't want you to have to worry about some of the hard things in life that happen if you don't take care of your body. Some girls think the way to look beautiful is to wear very short skirts and tight-fitting clothes and that they would look even more beautiful if they pierced their navel or nose or other parts of their bodies and wore rings in them. Some think a tattoo would make them more beautiful. Others think that wearing lots of makeup will make them appear cool or help them get lots of dates. How about you? Do you think you'd want to have friends who like the *outside* of you—what you wear or how you look—or do you think you'd want friends who like the *inside* of you, your personality?

Hillary: I'd want them to like the real me, who I am inside.

Me, too! Our bodies are an important part of us, but we don't need to show them off. We need to take good care of them. You need to feed your body good food because a strong body is one of life's priceless possessions. If you take care of it properly, you'll be able to use your body to do the things you really want to do. It is useful for everything from walking through the halls at school to participating in sports. So how important is it to take really good care of our bodies?

Hillary: Really *important.*

Let's compare your body to a car for a minute because a good car can get you where you want to go and help you have fun, just like a good body. What's the coolest kind of car? What car would you like if you could have whichever one you wanted?

Response. [Hillary may name a specific car, or she may say something as simple as "a fast new red one." Assume she says "a Porsche."]

Okay, now let's say you just put a lot of stickers on that Porsche and decorated it and parked it in front of the house and bragged about it all the time and showed off in it by driving way too fast. Would this be good?

Hillary [help and clues]: No, it would look worse if I did too many things to it. It's dangerous to drive too fast, and if I just showed it off all the time, people would just think of me as my car instead of knowing me for myself.

Right. Exactly. Now what if you had that same car but you took really good care of it, kept it clean, changed the oil, parked it in the garage (where no one would see it, but it would be really safe), and never bragged about it or showed it off. Would that be better?

Response.

Hillary, how is your body like that beautiful car?

Hillary [help and clues]: It's better to take care of it and keep it clean than to show it off and try to decorate it or change it too much. It's good to keep clothes on it so others don't see it too much and so they don't think of my body but my real self.

Respecting and Protecting Our Bodies

As parents we should look for a good balance between telling our pre-eight children too much about sex and their bodies and telling them too little. We want them to know enough to appreciate and respect their physical capacities and to protect themselves from any kind of sexual harm, yet we don't want to worry or frighten them in any way or to create any kind of negative attitude.

During their early elementary school years and before the "big talk," parents should look for opportunities to help children both respect and protect their bodies—all in the positive context of appreciating and caring for their marvelous physical gifts. Sexual dangers should be brought up very carefully and with much emphasis on the fact that a very small percentage of people would ever hurt a child and that the vast majority of adults would help and protect a child.

DIALOGUE

Adam, your body is one of the most amazing possessions you have. Aren't the things that it can do incredible? What are some of the things your body can do?"

Adam: Eat, run, swim, play the piano, jump.

Good, Adam. The thing you want to remember is that our bodies are miracles. They can do so many things. Every part of our bodies and everything our bodies can do is a gift that we should be thankful for. What are some parts of your body that you're thankful for?

Adam: Eyes, ears, mouth, legs.

There are some parts of our bodies that we call private parts because they are so special that we keep them private rather than showing them to everyone. What are some of your private parts?

Adam [help, clues]: penis, bottom, testicles.

Good, and what private parts do girls have?

Adam [help, clues]: Breasts, vagina.

You know, Adam, it's amazing how many names these private parts have. And the things we do with these private parts also have a lot of names. Some of the names are just cute words that families some-times use. (Discuss words you use for bodily parts and bodily func-tions.) You're old enough now, Adam, to know and use the real words for all these things, the correct words that we've been using in this talk we're having. Why do you think it's a good idea to use the correct words?

Adam [clues and help]: The right words show respect for our bodies.

Right. You know, Adam, lots of kids (and grown-ups, too) don't un-derstand how important their bodies are, so they don't take very good care of them. What's the problem with that?

Adam: They're more likely to get sick or hurt, and they won't have as much joy from their bodies.

Also, some kids don't appreciate how cool their bodies are. They like to say disgusting things about the functions of the body. For some reason they think it's really funny to make jokes about private parts of the body or urinating or having bowel movements [use whatever words you and your child feel comfortable with], and they use words that sound kind of gross and almost make you think that there's something weird about some parts of your body or some of the things your body does. Have you heard any words that sounded rude or crude to you?

Response, discussion.

Adam, when you hear a word that you think has to do with our private parts, always tell me so we can talk about what it means, okay?

Adam: Okay.

A lot of kids use the wrong words because they don't know the right words. Since we know the right words, we'll use them. If we want, we can still use our family words for our private parts and for what they do, but let's not use the gross words, okay?

Adam: Okay.

Now here's something else you're getting old enough to know, Adam. Some of our private parts can do other things besides helping us to go to the bathroom—amazing, awesome things that help us have babies! And guess what? When you turn eight, we're going to have a really special, really grown-up talk about this, and you will be amazed at what a fantastic thing grown-ups can do with their private parts.

If Adam says, "Why can't you tell me now?" indicate that you want it to be a special surprise for his eighth birthday.

Now, Adam, we don't let people who aren't in our family see or touch our private parts because they are so special. You understand that, right?

Adam: Right.

In our family, Adam, when someone hugs you or kisses you or holds your hand, how does it feel?

Adam: Good.

It sure does! That's called good touching. How about when your friend pats you on the back or puts his arm around you and says "good job" after you kicked a goal in soccer—does that feel good?

Adam: Yes.

Sure it does. When friends or family or people we love hug us or pat us or put their arms around us, that is good touching. Now let me ask you, is there such a thing as bad touching?

Adam: If someone tried to touch your private parts?

Right. That would be a bad touch. What other kind of touch might not feel good?

Adam: If a stranger puts his arm around you or patted you.

Exactly, Adam. These are bad touches. If anyone ever tries to touch you in a bad way, what should you do?

Adam [help, clues]: Yell PLEASE DON'T TOUCH ME! really loudly and then come to you right away and tell you about it.

Good, Adam. You'll have thousands of good touches from family and friends and people who love you, and you'll probably never have a bad touch. But if you ever do, you know what to do.

———

NOTE TO PARENTS: For a more detailed discussion on abuse, see p. 98. (The discussion there is written for slightly older children but can be adapted for pre-eight children.)

———

A Children's Fable

A Read-Aloud Story for Children Five and Older

Our book *Teaching Your Children Values* created more requests for auxiliary materials than any of our other books. Essentially, parents were saying, "Fine, thanks for the book, but give us something that we can hand to our children, something that will teach them values—directly!"

In trying to meet these requests we explored everything from interactive CD-ROMs to animated videos. What we finally came up with was a set of dramatic audiotapes called "Alexander's Amazing Adventures"—one for each of the twelve values in our book. They are filled with excitement, music, and vicarious experiences through which listening children internalize "that month's value." We found that exciting audiotapes hold kids' interest and have the flexibility of being used in cars and on a Walkman. We also discovered that children who listen to them live the values in their heads along with Alexander, the hero of the series and the prince of a magical land called Inland.

The remarkable team of musicians and playwrights who produced the series just breezed through the values of honesty, courage, respect, self-discipline, and peaceability, but then they came to the value of fidelity and chastity. For a time they were stumped. The tapes were intended for children as young as four. How could they deal with a subject like this one without saying too much? As often happens with artists, a metaphor came to the rescue. They created an adventure about beauty and commitment that could be read and understood on different levels by children of different ages. Younger children could love the story for itself and become so familiar with it that, when they were older, the metaphor could be explained and the story could then be used to help them understand the importance of sexual restraint and responsibility and the beauty of exclusive marital commitment.

We asked one of the creators of the audiotapes, Marvin Payne, to adapt this particular musical drama to a read-aloud story for three- to eight-year-olds for inclusion in this book. We think reading it to your children will give you a nice reference point for talking more specifically about sex later on. Children who are familiar with the story will often figure out the metaphors themselves as they grow older.

The Marriage Roses

Adapted by Marvin Payne from an episode of "Alexander's Amazing Adventures" by Marvin Payne, Steven Kapp Perry, and Roger and Melanie Hoffman

Once upon a time, there was a little boy named Alexander and a little girl named Elinor who were good friends. But they didn't play together every day because they lived in two very different places. Alexander lived on a street a lot like yours and mine, in a town that looked a lot like where you and I live. But Elinor lived in an old and magical place called Inland, a place to be found in well-worn storybooks. In Inland, boys wore pointy hats with feathers stuck in them, and girls wore brightly colored dresses all the time. But both boys and girls wore tall boots and warm capes because the mountains and forests of Inland were full of adventures.

Elinor never came to where you and I and Alexander live, but every now and then, when the wind was blowing just the right song and the clouds for a moment slipped into just the right shape and the light sparkled through the dust in the air with just the right color, Alexander would look around and find himself suddenly standing in Inland! And before too many minutes passed, Elinor would come from behind a tree or over a hill or just walk up behind him and say pretty loudly, "Hi. I've been waiting for you."

"Elinor? Hey, where am I? And what's this in my hand?"

"Punch, silly. It's what we drink at weddings."

"Am I at a wedding? Who's getting married?"

"My cousin Elaine and her handsome sweetheart, Edgar."

Just then they heard the noise of three big drums booming and a whole bunch of little pipes tweetling a slow marching tune that made Alexander feel hushed and happy and a little bit frightened all at the same time. Elinor whispered, "They're starting the march to the garden."

Alexander now watched as the marriage march progressed toward the garden. Elaine and Edgar looked splendid, but Alexander was a little puzzled, because nobody had ever told him about how Inlanders get married. So as he watched, Elinor tried to explain as best she could how in Inland the bride and groom lead a long march to their own marriage garden. Alexander could see the little parade heading toward some stone walls down in the meadow, and he wondered what magical things might happen inside those walls. Elinor told him that the bride and groom would go inside, just the two of them, and plant two rose seeds, one from her parents' garden and one from his parents' garden. There had to be two seeds because these weren't going to be ordinary roses. They were marriage roses, the most beautiful and magical flowers of all.

In Inland, the new husband and wife spend some time together every day taking care of what they have planted in their own secret garden. Soon, two tender green shoots peek up through the earth, and as they grow toward the sunshine, they curl and twine around each other. They grow like one stem, but twice as tall and strong. After a good long time, one rose blooms. As long as the husband and wife weed and water and enjoy it and treat it tenderly, the bloom lasts, and the sweetness deepens.

And the color keeps on changing! When the husband and wife are laughing, the rose glows yellow. When they hope for something good to happen, it trembles orange, like an ember about to burst into flame. When they cry together, it darkens to purple and blue. And when they are happy, it pulses ruby red.

And there's even more magic! When it hears the music of the man and the woman singing together, the rose changes from gold to silver and back again, over and over, faster and faster until it shimmers white, flashing out every color in the song, like sunlight on water.

Just then somebody screamed as Elaine fainted and fell flat on the grass. Edgar swept her up in his arms and carried her quickly home to her cottage, with Alexander and Elinor hurrying along behind. As he laid her down on her bed, he slipped off her head the circle of roses she had been wearing like a crown. The whole room was heavy with the smell of dying roses, gifts from Edgar to Elaine. Roses hung from the doorposts and windowsills, and leaned out of huge vases on the table and by Elaine's bed. Suddenly she sneezed loudly, like a little explosion, and moaned.

Elinor whispered to Alexander, "Something's funny here."

"Funny? That didn't sound to me like laughing."

"No, I mean, all these roses look like marriage roses."

"What's wrong with that?"

"Well, you would never cut a marriage rose from its garden and take it somewhere else."

"Elinor, I think we should stop talking about flowers and try to find a cure for Elaine." He grabbed her hand, pulled her out the door, and ran with her through the woods.

"Where are we going?"

"Look! Through the trees! A medicine wagon!"

In Inland, horses pull medicine wagons from village to village, and the medicine men stop for a while near each village and sell not only cures for bellyaches and blisters and bald heads, but also bonnets and buttons and butterfly nets. It looked as if this one was selling flowers.

"Don't push! Don't shove! Get your marriage roses! Plenty for everybody!"

Elinor couldn't believe her ears! Selling marriage roses? She'd never heard of such a thing! The medicine man rattled on: "All the marriage roses you'll ever want, without the bother of finding a husband or wife and fussing around for years in some damp garden!"

Alexander didn't like the look of the medicine man. He was a little too tall, a little too thin; his mustache was a little too pointy and his hair a little too shiny. He stood on the back of his wagon, surrounded by bundles of roses, and shouted answers down to the people crowding below, each one holding out a handful of coins.

"What? You want one like the first one you bought? Sorry, they're all different. Don't you know variety is the spice of life? You, sir—back again, I see. What can I do for you?"

The young customer burst out with "ahh-choo!" and Elinor saw that it was Edgar!

"I'll take—ahh-choo—a dozen yellow ones."

"Edgar! What are you doing here?"

"Buying roses for Elaine. She's awfully sick, and these cheer her up."

Elinor looked at the roses. "But they're fading already!" she said, and Alexander added, "She had a roomful of them. Why does she need more?"

"They die quickly. Ah-ah-ah-ah-choo! I'd better hurry back with these!" And Edgar ran off, scattering sickly rose petals behind him. Almost as soon as the petals touched the ground, they withered like bits of dusty paper.

Something about that sneeze made Alexander very suspicious, and he slipped off quietly toward the medicine wagon. Elinor felt as though the sky were suddenly flat and gray and empty of birds. She slowly walked a few steps down the path that Edgar had taken. Lying off to the side was a rose that had slipped out of the bundle. Elinor picked it up and took a big, deep sniff.

All this time Alexander was tiptoeing around behind the medicine wagon, trying to peek inside. "Whatcha lookin' for?" said a big wheezy voice. Alexander spun around. Nobody was there! "Broof! Ka-ka-broof!" It sounded as though an enormous horse had sneezed—which is exactly what had happened. Alexander had forgotten that certain animals in Inland could talk, and here was the medicine man's horse talking to Alexander! "Well, I, uh . . ." mumbled Alexander. The horse just said, "Hope it's not roses. Ka-broof!" He sneezed again. "The medicine man has so many, he just feeds the extras t' me instead of lettin' me munch on good green grass. I think there must be somethin' wrong with 'em, 'cause I'm getting sick eatin' 'em."

"Where does he get them all?" asked Alexander.

"Oh, he's planted a big farm o' stolen marriage roses. People buy 'em cause they don't want t' grow their own. Course they got t' buy lots of 'em 'cause they die quick."

An idea was flaming up like a candle inside Alexander's head. Right then he heard a loud sneeze from off in the woods. He ripped a big thistle out of the ground and held it for the horse to eat. "Here—and thanks!" The horse blew his lips out in a big smile and said, "Oh, no! Thank *you!*" But Alexander was already running away as fast as he could toward his sneezing friend.

"Ah-choo!" Elinor shook all over, and the rose in her hand quivered at the sound.

Alexander came running from behind the noisy crowd and shouted, "Elinor! Drop that rose!"

"Ah-choo! Why?"

"It's poison!"

"Ah-choo! Poison?"

Alexander grabbed it and threw it as far as he could.

Elinor cried, "And Edgar's taking Elaine even more of them!"

Fairly flying through the woods after Edgar, Alexander had barely enough breath to gasp out his story to Elinor.

"Talking . . . to the horse . . . medicine man wasn't looking. . . . Roses are marriage roses . . . stolen and planted on a big farm. . . . Sells lots of them because they die so quickly. . . . Feeds them to the horse, even. . . . That's why he talked to me. . . . tired of eating poison roses . . . wants grass instead. . . . People think they can have marriage roses for a few coins. . . . Don't want to grow just one that will last. . . . Don't know they're poison when they're cut away . . . from their . . . roots."

Soon they were crashing through the cottage door. Edgar jumped up from Elaine's bedside. "Please! Quiet! Someone's sick in here!" Alexander and Elinor began scooping the flowers up in huge armfuls and throwing them outside.

"Elinor, what are you doing with Elaine's beautiful roses?"

"Edgar, these are poison!"

"What do you mean?"

"When you cut marriage roses from their roots, they're poison!"

"But she loves them!"

A weak little cry came from the bed. "Yes, I love them!"

"You'll like the living ones more!" Elinor threw a stack of dead stems to Alexander at the door, and he tossed them far into the yard. "Living roses won't hurt you! Wouldn't you let these go if it meant getting well and having the real thing?"

Edgar reached for Elaine's pale hand, and they looked deep into each other's eyes before they answered with one voice: "Of course. That's what we've always wanted!" Edgar saw in Elaine's eyes the tall walls and cool shadows of a secret garden, and she saw in his the beautiful thorny arm of wood that would someday raise one perfect blossom high against the sun.

They were still looking into each other's eyes when Alexander, still at the door, heard the wind blow, looked up, saw the clouds move, and perceived a certain light through the dust in the air. He quickly looked back inside the cottage. For just an instant he thought he saw everybody smiling at him, as though he had done something really quite wonderful! But then they disappeared, and he was home.

NOTE TO PARENTS: You will find many opportunities to refer to this story and to use parts of it as "conversation starters" in the years ahead. It is important that your child hears it several times and is familiar with its messages and meanings. Once this familiarity is in place you can refer to it in future discussions when you are talking with your child about the danger of using sex at the wrong time or in the wrong way or about how beauty can become ugly and dangerous.

2

The Age Eight "Big Talk"

This dialogue is the "epicenter" of a parent's communication with a child about sex. It's the talk in which the most information is given. But keep in mind that this dialogue is not complete in itself. It doesn't stand alone—it needs lead-ins and follow-up.

Building Excitement and Positive Anticipation

As we mentioned earlier, age eight is a "window" between the disinterest of very young childhood and the moodiness and unpredictability of prepuberty. (Again, if your child is over eight but under twelve, go forward boldly with this talk, but modify appropriately.) Most eight-year-olds are trusting, open, innocent, anxious to please, and fairly fascinated by the world around them. They simply haven't yet learned to be embarrassed, sarcastic, or cynical.

Depending on where they live, some kids have heard quite a bit about sex by the time they're eight; others have heard next to nothing. Still others have heard quite a lot but paid no attention to it. Regardless of how much they have or haven't heard, whatever is on their slate is written pretty lightly and can be erased or rewritten or corrected by a prepared, committed parent. (Note, however, that this book is not written for parents who have to deal with an abuse problem. Such situations usually require counseling and professional medical expertise.)

One of the greatest things about most seven- and eight-year-olds is their susceptibility to anticipation and excitement. Because of this it is possible to really pump them up, to build a positive and happy level of enthusiasm leading up to the "big talk."

Unless you have compelling reasons for starting earlier or unless your child is already older than eight, we suggest that you target and plan for the day or week of the eighth birthday for the "big talk." Pegging it to a birthday can help build the desired kind of positive, excited anticipation. (It also gives you a deadline so you won't put it off.) If your child is a little older than eight, pick or designate some other special day that is at least a few weeks in the future.

Try something like the following to get your child excited and prepared:

DIALOGUE

Jason, you are getting old enough to understand some really important things, so when you turn eight on your birthday next month, we are going to let you in on a very exciting secret. In fact, we're going to tell you about the most wonderful and awesome thing in the world.

Jason: What is it?

Respond with something like: Oh, we can't give you any clues. You'll have to wait until your birthday. But I can tell you this: I'm excited because this is really something fantastic, and it's going to be such fun to tell you about it.

Jason: Well, just tell me what it's about.

No, that would be too much of a clue. We want this to be kind of like a secret until you turn eight. You probably know a little about the thing we're going to talk about, but on your birthday we're going to share the whole secret. And it is really wonderful, really incredible! I can hardly wait. Let's figure out exactly how long it is until you turn eight.

Jason: I think it's about four more weeks.

You can start having this type of "buildup" discussion with your child anytime during the year he is seven—or earlier if questions prompt it—but a month or two before the eighth birthday, shift into higher gear and mention it briefly every week or so. Use positive words like "awesome," "beautiful," "special," "exciting," "interesting." Finish the discussion with a statement like: "It is a secret about a very grown-up thing that most kids won't know all about, but you will. You'll know all about it after your eighth birthday. And let me tell you, it is the most wonderful, awesome, incredible thing in the world!"

The Age Eight "Big Talk"

Planning

As the birthday draws close, let your child choose a special place to spend the evening "exclusively"—just the child and you (both parents if married). This is a time separate and apart from the birthday party, which you might want to hold earlier in the day. The evening is just for the two or three of you and is devoted to "the most beautiful and awesome thing in the world."

Help the child choose a quiet, conversation-friendly place like a nice restaurant with a private booth or perhaps a place in the country where you could take a nice drive in the car. At home by the fire or on a cozy sofa is fine, too, as long as you can have privacy and not be interrupted. If the child prefers an activity of some kind, do it early enough that you can still have the evening open for the "big talk."

Well before the special day arrives, make a visit to the library or bookstore and pick out the picture book you will use as an aid in your discussion. Many are available under categories such as "maturation" and "child sex education." Have the librarian or bookstore salesperson help you. You will likely find at least half a dozen to choose from, but it's best to choose one book rather than two or three. Our personal favorite is *Where Did I Come From?* by Peter Mayle. An alternative is *How Babies Are Made* by Andrew Audry and Stephen Schep. Both of these are candid and clear and have a nice tone of importance balanced with "lightness" so the subject doesn't seem oppressive. (See page 62 for additional information on these and other books.) Two books that we particularly don't like are *It's Perfectly Normal*, which seems to us to essentially tell kids that pretty much every imaginable form of sexual expression is fine, and *Dr. Ruth Talks to Kids About Sex*, which we find to be an absurdly permissive book that suggests, among other things, that kids take steps to keep their sexual thoughts and activities secret from their parents. Get familiar with the book you choose and "rehearse" once or twice with the suggested dialogue that follows.

DIALOGUE

Well, Kathy, we told you this talk would be about the most wonderful, amazing, beautiful, awesome thing on earth. Are you excited?

Kathy responds. Be positive and encouraging about every answer; make the child feel important and special.

Before we start, we just want to tell you how much we love you. You already know that, but do you really know how much we love you? Do you know we love you way more than our jobs or our car or our house or any of our friends? We love you more than anything, except maybe each other—did you know that?

Response.

And that's one reason we're excited to tell you this fantastic secret. Because it's about love and it's about you! Does that give you any clues?

Response. If Kathy has asked some earlier questions that you've deferred, refer to them and let her know that this talk is about the answers.

Actually, what we've been telling you for weeks is a clue—that this was going to be about something really amazing and awesome. What do you think is the most awesome thing on earth?

Let her mention some things. All answers are good.

Yes, an airplane is pretty awesome. What can it do? A whale? Yes— why? When a person is mentioned, say, Now I think we're getting the best answer. Why is a person the most awesome thing of all?

Response. Discuss all the things the body and mind can do.

Okay, if a person is the most awesome thing, then the most awesome secret would be how a person gets made. Let's think about that. We're all big now, but what did we all start out as? What were we when we were just born?

Kathy: Babies.

Have you seen a baby lately? Did he have all his parts—fingers, toes, little eyelashes, a little belly button?

Response.

Babies are pretty amazing, aren't they! We remember so well when you were a little tiny baby. You were so cute and special. And you had all your parts. You just had to grow bigger to become you. Do you remember when you were a baby?

Response.

Now here's the big question, Kathy. Where do you think babies come from?

The hospital.

Yes, but how do they get there?

Mommy's tummy.

Yes, but how did the baby get in Mommy's tummy?

Response. (Child may say "From God" or "From a little seed.")

Good, but do you have any idea how that little body got started in there? (Ask each question with awe and excitement, not as a test or a quiz. Respond positively to each answer by repeating it and seeing if the child will go on. Then when the response runs down, start a slightly different line of questions.) Who do you think should become parents? What kind of people would be the best parents?

Kathy [help, clues]: People who love kids and take care of them.

Why would that be important?

Kathy: Kids need love and a loving family.

Would it be important for a baby's mom and dad to love each other?

Yes, very important.

How do you show people you love them?

Tell them, do nice things for them.

Can you show people you love them physically—with your body, with your arms or your lips?

You can kiss or hug.

Exactly. And if a man and a woman are falling in love with each other, what kind of kissing might they do?

Kathy [help, clues]: Longer, more romantic kisses on each other's lips.

Good, Kathy. Now, did you know there is an even bigger, better kind of hug that a husband and a wife can do? It makes each of them feel really good and really loved *and*—this is the most exciting part—this special kind of a big hug is what can get a baby to start growing inside the mom. Isn't *that* exciting?

Response.

Now we have a book here with pictures and everything. It shows about the special big hug that mommies and daddies can have and about how it starts babies and about how those babies grow inside their moms. Are you ready?

Yes.

Let's have you read it, and we'll stop and talk about things as we go along, okay? Isn't this exciting?

(Read the book. If the child is a comfortable reader, let her read. If not, you read, or perhaps you can alternate. Go slowly; frequently ask what she thinks. Answer questions as they come up. Emphasize at every opportunity how amazing, how beautiful, how marvelous it all is.)

How did you like that, Kathy?

(Some children think the pictures in some of the recommended books are a little bit comical, but emphasize how "awesome" the actual process is. Be personal about how much it lets you show your love and how private and wonderful it is when you save it for just one special person. And isn't it amazing that a whole baby—a whole *person*—grows from just that one tiny cell?)

Did you know any of that before?

Response.

Which parts?

Response.

What have you heard about sex?

Response.

Do you think your friends know very much about this?

Response.

Sometimes when kids haven't learned about sex from their parents—maybe they've just heard stuff on TV or from their friends—they know only parts of it, and they really don't know how awesome or how special it is. So they sometimes joke about it or make fun of it, but it's just because they don't know all the things you know now. So when you hear something silly or weird about sex, just be glad you know the real truth about it. You can always come and tell me if you hear something you don't understand, okay?

Kathy: Okay.

How old do you think you have to be to have sex?

Response.

(Explain that puberty is something that happens "to kids a little older than you." It makes people grow bigger and stronger and also gets their bodies ready to have babies. Promise that you'll have another talk soon about puberty, about the amazing changes and good things "that will happen to you as you go from being a girl to being a woman" or a boy to a man.)

Even if a boy and girl had gone through puberty and are big enough to have a baby, do you think they should?

Kathy: No.

Why not?

Kathy: They're too young. They're not old enough to start a baby or to take care of one.

And do you think, with something this special, it might be better to wait and have sex with just the one person you love most—like your own husband?

Kathy: Yes.

Why?

Response.

Do you think the big, awesome kind of hug we talked about is pretty important and pretty special?

Response.

So would you want to do it with a lot of people or just with one really special person?

Kathy: One really special person.

Kathy, remember that when we started, we said this would be a talk about love and about you?

Kathy: Yes.

Well, someday you will fall in love with someone and want to be with him all the time, and you'll want to share all your love with that person. Do you think it would be a good idea to save that big special hug—as you know, the short name for it is "sex"—for someone totally special?

Kathy: Yes.

So do I! We love you so much, and it's because of this wonderful thing called sex that you will someday have a child to love as much as we love you. Maybe when your little son or daughter is eight, you'll have this kind of talk with him or her. Do you think so?

Response.

Kathy, you'll hear a lot about sex in the next few years. Some of it will be good, but some will be pretty mixed up since a lot of people don't know the awesome stuff we've told you today. Anytime you hear anything that bothers you or makes you have a question in your mind, ask us, and we'll give you the answer. Will you do that?

Kathy: Okay.

The big special hug is called lots of things. Probably the best one is "making love," because two people should really, really love each other before they do it, and it's a way of making the other person know how much you love him. Sometimes the big special hug is called "having sex." Sometimes it's called other silly or even dirty names, like "screwing" or a word that we call the "f" word because we don't even like to say it. Have you heard any of those words? How did they make you feel?

(If the child says yes and something similar to "kind of weird," say something like:) Usually people who use those words aren't really thinking about how beautiful and awesome sex should be. And when kids use those other words, they're just trying to sound grown-up or cool, or maybe they just haven't been told all the things we've told you about.

So, Kathy, when you hear words like that in music or on TV or from other kids, just realize they're probably not thinking about what it means, that they might not know about all the good stuff.

Why would it be kind of bad for you to use words like that?

Kathy [help, clues]: Because I know the real words and because I know sex is too beautiful and special to make fun of or tell weird jokes about or even to use disrespectful words when we talk about it.

Now, "making love" or "having sex" doesn't always start a baby, but it should always show how much a man and woman love each other, and it shouldn't happen unless they are committed and loyal to each other. Do you know what those two words mean? What do you think loyal means?"

Kathy [help and clues]: Caring about someone, supporting that person, keeping promises.

What do you think commitment means?

Kathy [help and clues]: Being true to someone. Loving the person more than anyone else. Staying with the person. [Help her see that marriage is all about loyalty and commitment, and that the best way to show loyalty and commitment is through marriage.]

Why would it be a bad idea to have sex with someone you didn't feel committed and loyal to?

Kathy [help and clues]: It's just too special. If you did it with other people, it wouldn't be as special with the one you loved most. You wouldn't be loyal or committed to the one you loved.

Right. One other bad thing about having sex with just anyone is that there are some pretty bad sicknesses that people can catch. Have you heard of AIDS? (Explain as much as you think is appropriate, but don't go too far or cause worry or fear. Continue to get back to the essence—that sex, unless misused, is the most beautiful and awesome thing and that the reason for saving it is that it is so special.)

It's been so great to have this discussion with you. (Conclude with your arm around your child. Hold her close. Let her feel your love.) It's great that you're old enough to know about something this awesome. It makes me feel really close to you to have this kind of talk. I think you and I could talk to each other about anything, don't you?

Response.

Sometimes, as kids get older, they start thinking their parents don't understand them, so they don't talk about what they're thinking or what they're worried about. Do you think that will ever happen with us?

Response.

We'll be sure it doesn't! We'll trust each other and talk about everything, especially when we're worried about something or don't understand something. That's what families are for!

Brief Introduction to Eight Read-Aloud
Picture Books for Children

Where Did I Come From? by Peter Mayle. Just the right mix of seriousness and humor for an eight-year-old. One of the few books that really talks about "the big special hug" that can get babies started. (New York: Lyle Stuart, 1986.)

How Babies Are Made by Andrew Audry and Stephen Schepp. An older book but with good clarity and a nice warmth and feeling. Paper cut-out art substitutes for photos or drawings. (Boston: Little, Brown & Co., 1984.)

Where Do Babies Come From? by Angela Royston. Flowers, ducks, kittens, and people . . . all coming from seeds that grow. No reference to actual sex. A very basic book for pre-eight-year-old children with questions. (New York: DK Publishers, 1996.)

Being Born by Sheila Kutzinger. Again, nothing on sex or intercourse, but good on the growth and development of babies. (New York: Putnam & Grosset, 1992.)

The Wonderful Story of How You Were Born by Sidonie Gruenberg. Another old classic with lovely drawings. (Garden City, NY: Doubleday, 1970.)

How Was I Born? by Lennart Nilsson and Lena Swanborg. Interesting because a five- or six-year-old narrates in simple terms, and additional detail is separated in italics. Particularly good for a child about to have a younger sibling. Photography (especially of developing fetus) is beautiful. (New York: Dell Publishing, 1996.)

Mommy Laid an Egg! or Where Do Babies Come From? by Babette Cole. Tries a little too hard to be humorous with some things, such as sexual positions, but children will like it because parents give silly explanations of where babies come from, and their kids tell it like it is. (San Francisco: Chronicle Books, 1996.)

"Booster" Discussions

Some parents may read this heading and think, "Oh, no—*more* discussions? It's hard enough just to get through the 'big one.'" Actually, once you have had the age eight discussion, sex will be a far easier subject to approach with your child. In fact, if anything, some eight-year-olds want to discuss it too much—and with just about everyone. We'll never forget an experience with one of our sons at a Cub Scout banquet, just after his eighth birthday. He was seated at the other end of a long banquet table, and when we looked over at him during dessert, we noticed that he was the center of attention: Every other Cub Scout around him was leaning in, listening attentively, as Josh held court with his newfound wisdom. And it wasn't in the hushed tones of some joke or dirty story, it was expansive, open, excited, as if he were talking about the most wonderful, awesome thing in the world! Needless to say, we had forgotten the part of our discussion that suggested privacy and discretion.

The point is that once an eight-year-old has the positive orientation of the big talk, subsequent discussions are not difficult. In fact, you will find it enjoyable to administer a few "booster shots," or follow-up discussions.

Use the pattern presented in the two sample dialogues below. You may wish to ask the questions in the first dialogue independently of each other, using one whenever the moment presents itself, or you may want to go through them together as the agenda for a second or third major discussion.

Questions and Feelings

DIALOGUE

James, it's been a couple of weeks since your birthday and our special date. How have you been feeling about that awesome stuff we talked about?

Response.

Isn't it amazing how babies start and grow and become real little people inside their moms?

Response. Expand, appreciate, and respond to any observation kids make or any answer they give.

And don't you think it's cool how the dad's sperm and the mom's egg get together so the baby is kind of like the mom and kind of like the dad?

Response.

The best part is that it all gets started with that big special kind of hug we talked about. What do you think about that big special hug? Does it seem pretty neat to you?

Response. It's important to get more than one-word answers on these questions. You want to know how your child feels about what you discussed. Ask small related questions until you sense what he or she feels. If the child feels anything is strange or "gross" or "weird," do some reassuring.

You probably feel that a little because it's so new to you. But as a dad (mom) let me tell you that big hug is the greatest. It feels really good, and it lets your wife know you really love her and want to be with her for a long time. You'll feel that someday with the person you really, really love! James, from what I'm saying, can you feel how special and cool I think it is?

Response.

You know, James, I was just wondering if, since our talk, you've heard other kids talking about sex in some way or if you've heard or seen anything about it on TV.

Response. If James has heard something "dirty" or "weird" at school or from peers, carry on as follows.

You know, James, kids who don't know all that stuff we talked about just don't understand how wonderful and awesome sex can be. Since they only know parts of it, they can be a little confused and think sex is gross or weird. If they knew all that you do, do you think they would think it was cool and awesome?

James: Probably.

And then they wouldn't tell jokes or be silly or laugh about it, would they?

James: No.

(If your child has seen something on TV, ask him to explain what happened and to say whether he thought it was good or bad. Depending on what it was, what the child thought, and what your objective is, say something like:)

You know, one problem with TV or movies is that sometimes they show sex happening too soon, before people are really in love and really committed and loyal to each other. What is the problem with this?

James responds. Help him get back to the idea that it should be saved for someone really special—when there is commitment. Perhaps it didn't show how those people might feel the next day or in a year, or if one of them got sick, or if a baby started to grow, and so forth.

James, you'll hear a lot about sex in the next few years—from your friends, on TV, in movies, in music. Some of it will be pretty mixed up, and sometimes you'll hear words and things you've never heard and don't understand. Always come and tell me what you hear, and we can have these special talks about it—just you and me—so you'll understand everything. Okay?

James: Okay.

How much do you think your friends know about what we talked about on your birthday?

James responds. Help him see that different families talk or don't talk in different ways, but in this family we always try to be honest and open and talk about everything!

Family (Our Family Now and Your Family Later)

Whenever possible in our discussions with our children, we should connect sex with family. Children can understand quite readily and quite naturally that sex is best (and most natural and most important and most special) when it happens within marriage. They can also learn that saving sex can make families stronger. Here is one discussion approach:

DIALOGUE

Harmon, who are the most important people in the world to you?

Harmon: My family and my friends.

Good. Who are the people you probably love the most in the whole world?

Harmon: The people in my family.

Can you imagine ever loving anyone even more than your brother or your mom or dad?

Harmon: No.

But you know that someday you'll probably have a wife and children, and believe it or not, in some ways you'll love them even more. You'll have two families. The family you have now *and* the family you'll have later. Now, Harmon, what does sex have to do with families?

Harmon [help and clues]: It's how babies get started in families.

Right. Anything else?

Harmon [help and clues]: It's how couples show their love—they show that they love one person more than anyone else.

Harmon, how long do you think a family should last?

Harmon: As long as possible.

Why?

Harmon: Because we need families; we need their love.

We do! Divorce comes into many families, and people get separated by where they're living or what they're doing. But we're always linked to our families, aren't we? Especially to our own parents and our own children and our own husband or wife if we're married. How long can these relationships last, do you think?

Harmon: All our lives. Forever, I guess.

Can sex have anything to do with how long a family lasts?

Harmon: I don't know.

Let's think about it. If a married couple had sex only with each other, would it help their marriage feel safe and loyal and committed so it would last?

Harmon: Yes.

And what would be the opposite of that?

Harmon [help and clues]: If they had sex with other people, they could lose that feeling. They wouldn't trust each other, and maybe the marriage wouldn't last.

That's right. Do you know what it's called when two married people love only each other and make love only with each other?

Harmon [help and clues]: Being faithful or having fidelity. [Be sure he also knows what these words mean. Also reintroduce the words "loyalty" and "commitment" and what they mean in this setting.]

Right, being faithful or having fidelity. So what do these words mean?

Harmon: Having sex only with each other.

Harmon, it's the happiest and the safest way to live. That's how I hope it is for you, because I love you and want you to be the happiest you can be. Do you think that sounds pretty important—to be faithful to your wife once you find her and marry her?

Harmon: Yes.

Now here's a hard question, Harmon. Do you think you could be faithful to your wife before you married her, before you even know who she is?

Harmon: I don't know. How?

Well, there's an interesting song about that [from "Alexander's Amazing Adventures," the Eyres' values series mentioned on page 42–3]. Here, let's read the words to it out loud and see if you know what it means:

Faithful to a Dream

Where in the world, where can she be?
Maybe she's out there, dreaming of me.
Wondering my name,
The things that I do,
All of the things I wonder, too.

Faithful to a dream,
Faithful to someone I've never seen.
Someone who's out there, trying to be
Faithful, faithful to me.

What do you think that means?

Harmon [help and clues]: I guess you can have a dream about the kind of person you want to marry and be faithful to that dream even before you meet that person.

Why would that be good?

Harmon [help and clues]: It would make your marriage last longer?

Probably. Why?

Harmon: Sex would be more special and more beautiful and awesome, and you would trust each other more.

That's a good dream, isn't it Harmon!

A WORD FROM THE EYRE CHILDREN

We like the saying, "More parenting books should be written by children." Indeed, no matter how much we, as parents, think about and care about our kids, unless we get inside their heads a little and really know what they're thinking, we can miss the mark.

Since we've been through this "age eight discussion" nine separate times, and since each of our nine children is unique and different from the others, we thought we'd give them a chance to respond and give you the opportunity to read their recollections. What they say here will also introduce our children to you so that we can include other comments from their talks in the book.

Believe us, our children are far from perfect. Some are incredibly strong-willed and insist on sorting out everything for themselves, pretty much independent of our input. One or two are very shy, and it took some real effort to make the discussion a dialogue rather than a monologue. Some required a lot more "follow-up" and "monitoring" than others. But, amazingly, the early talks about sex we had with each of them really worked in terms of forming positive attitudes and avoiding early, casual sex. And they worked in terms of developing a closeness and a trust that carried over into other subjects and other aspects of our relationship.

The responses from our children that follow are almost completely unedited. We simply asked them to write a paragraph or two about their recollection of the talk we'd had with them on their eighth birthday. We gave them no other instructions. Some wrote in the form of a letter to us, others wrote as though explaining to a third party. We were amazed how much they remembered, how much of the detail and how much of their own feelings.

From Charity, age eleven, sixth grade, reads voraciously, plays the flute and plays soccer:

> *I remember, before I had the "big talk," I knew the most beautiful, wonderful, and amazing secret we were going to talk about was sex. The problem was that I didn't know what sex was. I was begging my dad for a clue, and about an hour before we left for the "big talk," he told me to think about how babies were born. "Babies are born by sex?" I thought. It was a little shocking to me, but I was very glad that I had a good idea of what we were going to talk about.*
>
> *My mother and dad took me to a totally nice restaurant called LaCaille (my choice). I remember that we sat at a little table outside and went through a book called* Where Did I Come From? *As I read it aloud, I did not know what to think, but it was very interesting to me. After a while I, too, believed it was the most wonderful, beautiful, amazing thing in the world. Then we went into the restaurant and ate and talked about it. I felt good inside.*
>
> *After the talk and still now, I feel so privileged to have my parents as my teachers in sex. I feel good that I know how wonderful it is. My friends find out as they grow but don't know the details or how great it is. Some of them consider it as something gross or disgusting. I consider it GREAT!*

From Eli, age thirteen, starting ninth grade, straight A student, a sports fanatic:

> *Growing up with seven older siblings, I had always heard about them having their "most beautiful, awesome thing in the world" talks. I never had one clue what it was about. I always thought it was a tropical flower or some kind of plant. Before I was eight I never really knew anything about sex or what it was.*
>
> *When I finally turned eight, I was excited to have the*

big talk. I was excited to be able to pick what restaurant I wanted to go to. At the time we were up at Bear Lake in Idaho. We drove into the nearest town called Montpelier and went to a restaurant called Butch Cassidy's. I remember ordering my favorite dinner, a chicken-fried steak. The restaurant was very crowded so we didn't stay long. We got in the car and drove to the grocery store so my mom could get some groceries. Then she came back out to the car and we had the "big talk." Before I had turned eight I had heard a little bit about sex from older kids and from movies and TV. I was still very unclear on what it was though. My parents had a book called Where Did I Come From? *which kind of aided them in teaching about sex to most of the kids in the family. I think the main point made was how special it was and how to save it for marriage. I was glad to learn about it at an early age so I didn't get the wrong impression from friends, TV, and movies about how sex is a bad thing. I think it is great now that everyone has learned about sex in our family that we can have talks about it and not feel awkward or uncomfortable.*

From Noah, age sixteen, sophomore class president and genuine leader but spaced out enough to keep everyone laughing:

Well, my parents told me that when I was eight, I could learn about the most beautiful thing in the world and that I could choose where to go for dinner. (I chose the Training Table, by the way, and we had to move a few times to avoid people and have privacy.)

Man, I was excited. I had no idea what for. Honestly, I imagined it being about some great unknown place or something. So I was shocked. Interested though.

I now value the fact that I was taught about sex in that setting. After that "talk" and several follow-up conversations on the subject I felt like I could and feel like I can talk to mis padres *(my parents in* español*) about anything. I realize why my parents had called it the most beautiful,* *wonderful, amazing thing in the world. At first I couldn't understand why they didn't add "weird" in there. But when I was taught what joy and happiness it could bring to your life when you save such a special thing for your wife, it all came together.*

From Talmadge, age eighteen, high school all-American basketball player, and an artist and architect:

Well, to tell you the truth, it never really registered to my mind what sex was until you and Mom told me. You both were building it up to be some amazing thing called "the most beautiful thing in the world," so I was excited to hear what it was but I had no clue of what it might be.

You've got to remember that I was quite sheltered. I was a quiet boy who was living in England, and the only people I'd hang out with were my brothers and my friend Matt.

We went to an Indian restaurant. I remember it was quite dim in there and that Mom was telling Dad to keep it down because others could hear us. Then you pulled out that book that helped you explain it. I found it quite interesting, but being that age it didn't tie into a thing I thought about every day. To tell you the truth I was more interested in trading cards and go-carts than sex.

The main thing I remember during the talk was that my parents were giving me their full attention. That was rare. It was my night. This does not happen too often with a family of 9 children. I felt good because I knew that my parents cared about me, and I could tell that this thing they were telling me was important to them and me.

It has always been so good to know the things you guys told me that night. Later, when friends would talk about sex, I just felt like I knew all about it and knew that it was (could be) beautiful.

P.S. I was clueless when I was 8, but there are a few people who I know that are 6 or even 5 and they know all about it. I believe in your "8" thing, but are there exceptions?

From Jonah, age nineteen, college sophomore, loves the outdoors, loves people; writing from London:

I remember the day well! There was the great mystery factor. We traveled in silence to the little restaurant I'd chosen where we got a fairly private booth, and Mom and Dad poured it all out. We went beyond the basics because I had lots of questions. We talked about the slang words and the proper words. We talked about periods, masturbation, everything . . . well, not everything. There are some things I was nowhere near ready for, but it seemed like everything at the time.

Sex became a word that could be spoken freely and an open subject between my parents and me. It had such a positive meaning in our home, unlike here in England where that three-letter word on the front page sells so many magazines and newspapers.

Sex is so powerful, it creates life and it strengthens love. I remember we talked about the horse comparison—so strong, so beautiful, but needing to be bridled and controlled. I think that age eight talk acted like a bridle. Those two or three hours were the foundation for how I feel now (about the most beautiful thing in the world).

From Saydi, age twenty-one, senior at Wellesley, on leave doing humanitarian work in Madrid, Spain:

I have a terrible memory, but surprisingly I remember many of the details of my "8 year old talk." I remember being in big-time anticipation to learn the secret that my four older siblings prided themselves in knowing. And when the day finally arrived to learn about the "most beautiful thing in the world," I was so ecstatic and in the air that I left my brand-new bike in the middle of the driveway and on the way out my mom ran over it. She told me that we would have to postpone the talk, and I was absolutely devastated. I guess my parents did a good job at building up the anticipation. I literally couldn't wait to get in on this secret.

I was in for a surprise when I learned what it was all about. As they unfolded things to me in our private booth in the restaurant, I was a little shocked—but more than anything I remember feeling like they were trusting me with a grand secret—some correct and top secret information about something that most of my friends didn't understand completely or correctly.

I also remember them telling me that I could talk to them about it anytime—if I had questions or problems—it was an open topic—I think that helped my relationships with my parents—they are my best friends in the whole world—being away from home I miss talking to them and asking their advice more than anyone else.

From Josh, age twenty-three, college senior, heading for graduate work in architecture; spent two years in voluntary service and study in England:

Eight years old for me was a long time ago—fifteen years to be exact. I don't remember a lot from that time, but one of the things I do remember was the important discussion I had with my parents the night of my eighth birthday. They had been telling me for several weeks that on that special night they would talk to me about the most wonderful thing in the world. I remember wondering what they thought the most wonderful thing in the world was. "Maybe they are going to talk to me about how I shouldn't fight with my little brothers and sister," I remember thinking.

The night of the discussion finally came. Me and my parents sat on the couch in the living room of our house in Virginia. I saw that my dad had a book called, Where Did I Come From? *and I thought, well, maybe this will be interesting. They asked me about school and my birthday, and then we got into the discussion. They kind of went through an introduction, telling me about falling in love, and Dad then started reading the book to me. This book was a very good aid in the discussions because it explained things very clearly and it had good drawings.*

After the discussion I felt like I knew more about life than anyone in my school. I felt really privileged that my parents had had that talk with me, because I knew that most of the other kids would never have a talk like that with their parents. I felt like I knew one of the greatest mysteries of life—how a baby starts growing in its mommy's tummy. And I was grateful to my parents for making the discussion so special to me.

My "age eight discussion" made me realize that I could talk to my parents about just about anything.

From Shawni, age twenty-five, Boston University; spent eighteen months working in an orphanage and doing other humanitarian and voluntary work in Romania. She and husband, Dave, work at the Points of Light Foundation in Washington and are the parents of baby Max:

I have to admit that I really don't remember being very curious about where babies came from when I was eight. I guess it just made sense to me that moms could have babies. But I do remember all the excitement around the "special talk" my parents kept saying we would be honored and privileged to have when we turned eight. The "talk" was going to be about "the most beautiful, wonderful, awesome thing." Saren got the talk before I did, and I was pretty excited about being next in line.

Although my memories of the details of the talk are vague, I do remember quite perfectly the feeling that was in the room as we talked. My parents told me about "where babies come from" with perfect candor but also with a great deal of love and respect. I really remember that feeling of love and how special this whole thing was.

The whole concept made sense to me. I remember feel-

*ing comforted that my parents would take the time to tell
me about that—and a little embarrassed—but mostly it
just felt right and good and natural.*

From Saren, age twenty-six, B.A. from Wellesley College and
M.A. from Harvard, eighteen months in Bulgaria. Recently
started a new company in Boston developing and marketing
new curriculum and educational approaches:

*When I was seven years old, I began to wonder why
fathers seemed to be an integral part of so many families.
I had several younger brothers and sisters, so I'd seen my
mother's protruding belly with each new child and had felt
the unborn baby kick around in there when I placed my
hand on my mother's tummy. I had a basic understanding
of the fact that babies come out of their mothers. But I
didn't get how fathers fit into the picture. I loved my
dad—he was a whole lot of fun, but was he necessary?
What made me distinctly his daughter rather than someone else's daughter? How was I really connected to him?*

*Anyway, I asked my parents why babies needed dad-
dies and how you know what daddy should go with what
baby. And they said I had some really good questions and
they had a lot of great stuff to explain to me, but I'd have
to wait a couple of months for my eighth birthday. Then
we'd have a big talk. (That may be how our family's age
eight tradition got started. As the oldest child, I asked the
questions when I was seven, and they put me off long
enough to summon their courage and get their act together.) As the weeks went by, my parents kept telling me
that they were getting really excited for the big talk we were
going to have when they were going to tell me about "the
most wonderful thing in the world."*

*My eighth birthday finally rolled around, and after all
our celebrations and after the little kids were put to bed,
my parents sat down with me by the fireplace in the living
room and used this book with cartoon people and a nice*

dosage of humor called Where Did I Come From? *to explain to me the basics of sex. I could tell that they were a bit nervous; after all, I was the oldest so this was their first time explaining all this to a kid. But they not only told me about the basic "plumbing" of sex, they told me that it was a wonderful, special thing that two people who loved each other could share. I don't remember the exact words they used, but I remember the basic feeling of the message, and it was good and warm.*

We hope you enjoyed those candid recollections as much as we did. We realized as we read what they wrote—realized more than we ever had before—that the talks really worked, that they had some impact and made some difference. And if you really knew our kids—knew how obstinate and impetuous some of them are, how private and hard to talk to some of them sometimes are, how into pop culture and prone to be influenced by peer groups others are—you'd know that this discussion, if approached carefully and courageously, can work with anyone.

Reading those recollections made us appreciate our children all the more and made us realize again that those were far more than little talks about sex. They were what our friend Stephen Covey calls "deposits in the emotional bank account." They were trust and communication builders; they were intimate discussions about intimate things that showed our love for them and our hopes for them. They were a way to be exceptionally close.

3

Follow-up Talks with Eight- to Thirteen-Year-Olds

Think of the "big talk" and "boosters" as a firm foundation.
Having them in place allows you—actually empowers you
as a parent—to build on it, to install the walls and roof
and windows and skylights of "the most beautiful
thing in the world."
Over the next four or five years, as your child progresses
toward adolescence, additional related discussions should be
used to expand his understanding and to recommit him to
correct principles. Samples of these "implementing"
discussions are outlined in the pages that follow.

Middle-Aged Kids

The discussions in this chapter are aimed at and developed for kids between the ages of eight and thirteen, between the conceptual and interest threshold that comes at about eight years and the changes of puberty that come in early adolescence. We call this important but often neglected age span the "middle age" of childhood.

In a way it is a magic time and certainly an opportunistic time for parents. Middle-aged kids are usually extremely curious and interested. They are conversational and conceptual enough to understand most of what is explained to them. They are flattered by responsibility and by being treated as grownups. They are not yet emotionally or hormonally preoccupied with sex, so they can mentally take a step back and look at sex objectively. And at this age they don't yet, for the most part, have the cynicism, sarcasm, and skepticism that lurks just around the corner in full-fledged adolescence. In short, it is the optimal time to teach a lot of value- and character-related things as well as intellectual things.

This eight-to-thirteen span is an age range that we don't focus on enough as parents. Take a look at the child care section in a big bookstore sometime. You'll find hundreds of books on babies and preschoolers, and hundreds more on teens and adolescents, but very few on kids in between. We tend to worry more about the little ones and the big ones. The problems, the needs, and the concerns are just more obvious in these groups. We worry about how our preschoolers are developing, learning, and growing, and we worry about what our teenagers are thinking, drinking, and doing. The middle-aged kids are usually less trouble, less worry, so we often leave well enough alone. In doing so we miss a golden opportunity to help establish the self-esteem, character, and understanding that will go far toward ensuring a happy and productive life.

When parents go on the offense with middle-aged kids,

they often avoid being constantly on the defense with adolescents and teenagers. If we teach our children what to do in the eight-to-thirteen window, we'll spend less time telling them what not to do later. And the trust level and communication patterns we set up before adolescence will carry into the teen years, the period when parent-child understanding often dries up.

For example, it's rather hard to imagine a fifteen- or sixteen-year-old going to his or her parent and asking for input or advice on a sexual question, incident, or dilemma unless it has been a subject of trust and communication for several years. If the discussions that follow are used with adolescents, they will have to be modified, and parents should expect it to be harder and take longer than with a middle-aged child who, among other attributes, might still believe that you know something.

The suggested dialogues and discussions in this section are arranged in what we think is a fairly natural chronological sequence—that is, according to the ages they work best. The discussion that could happen as early as eight or nine comes first, and discussions more relevant to twelve- and thirteen-year-olds come last. Again, the ages are "suggested" or "ideal," which doesn't prevent the discussions from working effectively with older or sometimes younger children. The sequence in which they are presented here is rather important, though, since most of the later discussions will not be as effective if they are not preceded by most of the earlier ones. Still, within those guidelines, it's best to have each discussion when someone or something brings it up naturally a question, something in the media, a peer group situation, or something the child heard or noticed.

All of the follow-up discussions presented in this section should happen by the time your child enters adolescence and puberty. Then you are in on the ground floor: You, as the parent, have had the "first word" on each important aspect. All that your child sees and hears and experiences of sex in the years ahead will have a chance of falling within the positive framework you have built. This also preserves open communication, allowing you to advise your child on the sex-related scenarios and situations that will come during adolescence and beyond.

In other words, if you have these suggested early, preemptive discussions about sex with your child and thus establish the direction of your child's thinking, then subsequent sex-related messages or situations or circumstances that could otherwise be problematic will become opportunities for further discussion and for reemphasis of what is best and what is not.

Never Let the Subject Become Inactive: Media and Peer Group "Triggers" for Discussions with Eight- to Thirteen-Year-Olds

We've known parents who had highly successful "big talks" with their eight-year-olds, heaved a sigh of relief, and never raised the subject again. Instead, we think of the age eight discussion as the opening of a door to a place that we want to be always accessible and frequently visited. Once you have "equipped" your child with a clear and positive introduction to both the facts and the commitments of sex, he or she will be aware enough of the subject to have plenty of questions come to mind—questions that he may not ask unless you make sure there are plenty of easy opportunities to do so.

One key way to stay on the offense is to take the very two influences that parents fear most for their children—the media and the peer group—and use them to create ongoing follow-up discussions. We suggest two media approaches and two peer group approaches.

Media

Take the time to watch a sitcom or two with your child or to watch whatever he or she likes on TV. It is almost a certainty that parts of the plot or dialogue will have sexual references or implications. When the show is over, ask "opinion" questions: "Did people do the right thing?" "What did some of the words they used mean?" "Do you think they 'get it'— about sex being the most beautiful thing in the world?" The same kinds of discussion can also be generated by thumbing through a current magazine together. Even the sexual innuendo of the advertisements leads to good follow-up discussions.

Or you can take a more general approach: "What are your favorite TV shows or movies?" "Do they have anything at all about sex in them?" "Did you hear any words or see anything about sex that you didn't understand?" "Well, you know, now that we've had our big talk and everything, whenever you see or hear anything about sex, tell me what it was and whether you understand it and whether you think it was okay or not okay."

Peer Group

When you're the "soccer mom" or the "pick-up dad," listen in on your kids' conversations. What are they talking about? Are there certain friends who bring up sexual subjects or use sexual terminology? How do other kids respond? Just by listening you'll often have the basis for a little private conversation later. "I sure like your friends. They're good kids. Which of them do you think knows about sex? Why do you think so? Billy talks a lot about it, doesn't he? What do you think of what he says?" Keep everything positive and nonjudgmental but take opportunities to remind your child that many other kids don't know all the details, so they're a little silly or a little gross about the whole thng. Always ask your child if she has any questions about anything she's heard.

The more general approach here would be to simply ask a few things when there is a private moment or two. "Now that you know all about sex, I'll bet you notice kids talking about it or using words about it sometimes. Do you?" "Which of your friends do you think knows the most about it?" "Do you think they've had a 'big talk' with their parents?" "Do you think they know how beautiful and awesome sex can be?" "Why do you think some kids make fun of it or tell jokes about it?"

Regardless of how you get these little incidental discussions started, the key is to use them as reinforcements of the same points made in the "big talk"—the beauty of sex, the miracle of it, the importance of it, and the "specialness" of it.

Making Decisions in Advance

We have one particular seminar discussion that we love to present to older kids (fifth or sixth grade) at elementary schools and middle school kids. You can adapt it into a point-by-point dialogue with your child. The sequence goes something like this:

1. As young as you are, and given our ongoing medical advances, your life expectancy is somewhere around eighty-four years. That means you will live seven life segments of twelve years each.

2. All of you are just starting (or about to start) the second seventh of your life. In your first seventh you went through your childhood and through elementary school.

3. Now, what do you think are the most important decisions you will make during your whole life?

(The first answers are usually about what profession to have, whom to marry, college—whether to go, where to go, what to major in, and where to live. Then a slightly different type of decision usually comes up: whether to do drugs, whether to be honest, whether to smoke, whether to have sex, whether to really apply oneself and do one's best.)

4. It's interesting that there are two kinds of decisions here. There's the "multi-alternative" kind, which we can't

make until we get a little older and know all the options, like whom to marry or what profession to pursue. Let's call these "category one decisions." The other type of decision is the "right or wrong" kind, just two alternatives—one is right, and the other is wrong. Let's call these "category two decisions."

5. Now let's go back to the thought about the sevenths of life. Here's the big question: In which seventh of life do we make most of life's most important decisions, category one *and* category two? (Kids realize quickly that virtually all of their most important decisions, the ones with the longest lasting consequences, will likely be made in the second seventh—the twelve-year period they are entering.)

6. Isn't that a little scary? You're so young in the second seventh, but you have to make the decisions that will determine how healthy, how successful, and how happy you'll be for the other five sevenths!

7. There is a way that you can make all of the important category two decisions (the right or wrong ones) *now* or in the next few days—and make *right* decisions on them. Then you'll never have to worry about them again, and you can save your energy and thought for the other important ones—the category one decisions where you'll have to think through lots of alternatives.

8. Here's how you do it. In a very special, very private place, like the back of your journal or diary, make up a list called *Decisions in Advance.* These are decisions where you can figure out right now what is right and what is wrong, and if you decide *strongly* enough and write that decision down, date it, and sign it, it can be like a contract and a promise to yourself. Any decision you write there and sign is *made,* and you won't ever have to decide it again. For example, if you decide (totally firmly, in advance, and in writing) that you won't do drugs, then you don't have to keep making that decision whenever someone offers them to you.

Most early adolescent kids, even in a large group setting, with a little help and encouragement can make a solid list of six or eight decisions in advance. In the more intimate setting of a family, with a parent's help, even stronger advance commitments can be made. These decisions can involve anything from "not smoking" to "going to college." Parents can make up little case studies or scenarios to clarify the advance decisions ("You're fifteen, and you're at a party where everyone is smoking. Even the girl you're there with is trying to get you to light up. What will you do? What will you say?") This kind of dress rehearsal prepares a child for the real event.

Decisions in Advance can be particularly useful (and powerful) with regard to sex. A young child who "gets it" about "the most beautiful, wonderful thing in the world" will want to make a decision to save sex for a time of true love and long-term commitment. Once this advance decision is written and signed in the child's private journal, it can be "revisited" as years go by, and a parent can help reinforce it through praise and perhaps through presenting scenarios about possible situations and helping the child rehearse what he would say or do.

Puberty Discussions for Nine- to Twelve-Year-Olds

Most public elementary schools teach "maturization" classes in the fourth or fifth grade, which is another good reason for the timing of the age eight parental discussion—to get a positive foundation laid before the bricks and boards of scary and random information start flying in from every angle with every kind of twist.

School maturation and sex education classes range from straightforward and useful to absolutely awful, depending on the teacher, the school district, the curriculum, the politics, and other factors. Horror stories abound, from the elementary principal who sent all his sixth graders a Valentine's Day card with a cute little verse about safe sex and a condom pasted inside, to the documented account in the October 1994 issue of *Atlantic Monthly* of a New Jersey high school teacher who said, "I teach that the key to good sex is lubrication. . . . I talk about sexual positions. . . . We talk about the taste of different people, how kissing tastes. . . . The topic leads to discussion of masturbation, how it feels to touch our genitals."

Thankfully, few parents will be faced with situations this extreme, and the purpose of this book is not to take political positions or to make judgments about school sex-ed programs. (Parents can, it seems, spend a great deal of time worrying about what others may say to their child about sex and very little time figuring out what to say themselves.) Rather, our purpose here is to put parents in a preemptive and preeminent position where they teach their children first and then actually use school maturation classes (just as they use media and peer group references to sex and sexuality) as starting points for ongoing discussions with their children. These discussions will then occur within the preset framework of sex as a beautiful and special gift to be used at the right time, in the right way, with responsibility and discipline.

Base the timing of your personal puberty discussion on when maturation or elementary sex-ed classes start in your child's school and on when you think the earliest aspects of your child's puberty will begin. Be sure you precede and supersede both. If you have already laid the groundwork through the "big talk," in which you mentioned the word "puberty" and explained it as the growth process that makes it physically possible for people to have sex and start babies, it is a fairly natural and rather exciting thing to watch for the right opportunities and interest level for you to elaborate.

DIALOGUE

Kate, I think you're about old enough to talk a little more about puberty, about some of the changes that are just about to start happening in your body as you go from being a girl to a woman. Are you up for that?

Response.

Have you heard anything about puberty since we talked about it?

Response.

How would you define "puberty"?

Response. Help her define it as the natural changes her body goes through as she becomes a woman. Be comfortable and help her be comfortable and conversant with such terms as "breasts," "pubic hair," "vagina," and "penis."

Kate, it won't be long before you'll start having some of these changes, and they are exciting. You'll get taller and stronger, your voice will get a little richer and more mellow, your breasts and hips will start to develop and grow, and hair will begin to grow under your arms and between your legs. And believe it or not, you'll actually start to like boys a little better. It's something to really look forward to. Some kids begin puberty earlier than others. Do you know some kids that are already starting?

Response.

When do you think puberty usually begins, and how long do you think puberty lasts?

Kate [clues and help]: It can start anytime between nine or ten and thirteen and fourteen, and most of it—the biggest changes—happen over a couple of years.

That's right, and it really doesn't matter whether you have a late or early puberty as long as you understand and appreciate what is happening to you. Puberty is exciting; you get bigger and stronger and better. It's all good, very good—well, except for maybe two little things. Can you think of a couple of things about puberty that might not be so good?

Kate responds. If she says something like "I don't want to grow up" or appears to have some fears, reassure her and tell her the positives again before going on.

Well, the two things I'm thinking about don't last and aren't that terrible, although they seem so at the time. One is complexion problems—pimples or acne. Some kids have to deal with this in puberty, but there are creams and stuff for it. And sometimes kids get little growth pains just because they are growing so fast. The other thing I'm thinking about affects everyone in puberty and those around them. It's called moodiness. During the two or three years while you're changing the most, you'll have some pretty interesting moods. Sometimes you'll feel totally happy and excited and up for no reason, and other times you'll feel depressed and stupid and down and not even know why you feel that way. The thing to remember is that everyone in puberty gets these moods. They usually don't last very long, and there isn't much you can do about the depressed or bad moods. Just kind of expect them, and then they won't bother you very much. Remember that, okay?

Kate: Okay.

Why do you think kids get things like pimples and growth pains and lots of extreme moods in puberty?

Kate [help and clues]: Probably just because they are growing so fast. Everything is changing, even the chemicals in their body.

Exactly right, Kate. Now let's talk about another really important thing that happens to girls during puberty. It's called menstruation or having periods. It's a really wonderful thing, but it can be kind of hard to adjust to and get used to. Have you heard of menstruation or periods before?

Response.

Well, remember when we talked about the egg that forms in a woman that can turn into a baby if a sperm from a man hooks up with it? Well, Kate, once a girl goes into puberty, at least one of those eggs gets released from her ovaries about once a month. The egg comes down the fallopian tube like the book showed, and if it is not fertilized by a sperm, it just keeps on going and comes out. It's too small to see, but some blood comes out with it and that blood is plenty big enough to see. So a woman, or a girl in puberty, bleeds a little once a month or so from her vagina. Do you understand?

Kate responds. Encourage her to ask questions. Go back to the picture book if you need to and tell her that she'll also learn about it in school.

The reason I said menstruation is a wonderful thing is that it shows things are working right in your body so you'll someday be able to have a baby. But bleeding once a month could be a little scary, don't you think?

Response.

All girls worry a little about it at first, but it's not as bad as you might think. There are little pads you can wear so nothing gets dirty, and you can just keep doing your normal activities. When this first happens to you, let me know and I'll show you exactly what to do so you won't have to be concerned, okay? (Clearly, this talk is best from mother to daughter, but there is no reason a father can't do just fine with it.)

Kate: Okay.

Periods or menstruation happens a lot earlier in some girls than others. It's nature's way of getting a woman ready for the time that will come years later when she will want to become a mom. What do you think of that?

Response.

What do you think of the whole idea of puberty?

Response.

What do think will be the best parts and the hardest parts of puberty?

Response. Follow up and discuss things reassuringly, always giving the feeling of trust, of respect, of being glad your child is mature enough to know and understand these things.

Kate, boys also change a lot during puberty, but they usually do it a little later than girls. If you've ever watched a bunch of sixth or seventh graders, most of the girls look a lot older than most of the boys. But the boys catch up. They get taller and stronger, their shoulders get broader, they even have to start shaving their faces, poor things. They get pubic hair, too, and their penises and testicles grow bigger. One kind of funny thing is that boys' voices change more than girls. They get deep all of a sudden, and sometimes it sounds like a completely different person talking. Any questions about that?

Response. Review as you feel is necessary. Be positive and praise every question or comment Kate has.

Kate, we'll keep talking about this. We haven't covered everything yet. But the main thing to remember is that I've been through puberty and remember it really well. That's why I want you to always tell me when you have questions or things begin to happen. I'll be as excited as you. It's really like a miracle. You change from a little girl into a young woman. It's even more cool than a caterpiller turning into a butterfly! I love you and am excited for you. I want to share the excitement, so I want you to let me in on everything. No secrets, okay?

Response.

Let me tell you something funny that happened to me when I was going through puberty about your age. (Children love hearing about experiences that happen when growing up, especially embarrassing ones and especially from a parent. Sharing a memory or two will increase the chances of the child's sharing experiences and feelings with you.)

If this discussion is with a boy, simply reverse the order of information. Boys usually don't need to know a lot of detail about girls' periods at this young age, but you should spend a few minutes on wet dreams and anything else that might otherwise surprise them.

Preemptive Talks on Connected Subjects: Birth Control, Abortion, Rape, Abuse, Prostitution, Masturbation, Homosexuality, AIDS, and Pornography

The key here is to discuss these subjects early enough to be preemptive (to have the information you give and the attitudes you project precede what your child gets elsewhere) and yet late enough not to create unnecessary worry or thrust children into something that takes away their innocence prematurely or that gives them information they don't need yet.

For most children this not-too-early-not-too-late window is somewhere in the ten-to-twelve range. If the subjects come up earlier (and come up seriously, with the child having real questions and interest), then go with this discussion earlier. Younger kids may have heard the words or may have heard or seen related things, but if it hasn't really registered or interested or concerned them yet, just wait. Still, if you're going to err, err on the too early side. Just be sure your discussion is positive and "light" enough that it doesn't create unnecessary concerns. Remember that the goal is to maintain the positive, respectful, beautiful attitude you have sought to establish about sex.

Make your own decision about whether to cover all the subjects here in one discussion. If your child is relatively young—eleven or under—you might want to cover only the words or concepts he has heard and is wondering about, saving the others for later. On the other hand, if he or she is twelve or older, you might want to go through them all on the assumption that those that haven't caught his attention yet soon will.

Here is a sample approach:

DIALOGUE

(Begin with a bit of a follow-up on the puberty discussions you've had already because ongoing puberty-as-it-progresses talks are necessary to keep the subject open and approachable. Expect a little embarrassment and resistance when you bring it up, but persist, letting your child know it's as important to you as it is to him.

Wyatt, it's been a few weeks since I asked you about puberty, and I've noticed how much you're growing lately. You look taller than you did last month. Have you noticed any of the other "signs" we talked about?

Response.

Any voice changes? Any new hair anywhere? Any wet dreams? Are girls starting to look a little more interesting to you?

(Do this good-naturedly, with your arm around Wyatt. The tone is one of interest, love, and pride in his growth and maturity. Reemphasize that it doesn't matter when those things happen. Early or late is just as good. You just want to share in the big events because they are exciting and important.)

As you get older, Wyatt, and as we keep talking about these things, you'll know even more what a great and awesome thing sex is. We'll talk about a lot of things that are related to sex that we want you to understand, including the meaning of some words that you may already have heard. Let's write some words on the left side of this piece of paper, and we'll write the definitions on the right side. Okay?

Wyatt: Okay.

(It's best for Wyatt to do the actual writing. Say each word and let Wyatt write it down and say if he has heard it and knows what it means. Explain that these are not bad or incorrect words like some of the ones you decided to try not to use in the "appreciation for bodies" and "pornography" discussions. These are just words that are about some of the things that happen to people and that have to do with sex. Some of the things they describe are bad and sad things, but the words are okay to use. Let Wyatt make definition notes on the right side of the paper. Say something about each italicized word.)

BIRTH CONTROL: Remember that there are two great reasons

for sex. One is to try to have a baby, and the other is to show a really special kind of love to one really special person. What are some reasons that people might not want a baby for a while? When people want to show that special kind of love but don't want to have a baby right away, there are things they can do to stop a baby from starting. The woman can take a *pill* that stops the egg from coming down or she can have a doctor put something called an I.U.D. inside her to keep the egg and sperm from getting together. The man can wear a *condom,* a tight little sleeve or tube over his penis that catches the sperm. All these things are called *birth control* because they try to control when a baby gets started and gets born. Since an egg comes along only once a month or so, some couples just try to figure out when that is and not have sex during that time each month. This is called the rhythm method of birth control. None of the birth control methods is foolproof or perfect. Sometimes people still get pregnant even when they're trying not to.

ABORTION: Sometimes if a woman has certain health problems, her doctor might tell her that being pregnant or having a baby could make her very sick, maybe so sick that she could die. In this situation, if a woman is trying not to get pregnant but still does, she might consider having an *abortion.* That is when a doctor operates and stops a baby from forming. It is usually done really early in the pregnancy, in the first trimester (the first three months, or the first third of the nine-month pregnancy, while the *fetus*—the tiny beginning of a baby—is still very tiny, smaller than your fingernail).

(Note: Where you go or don't go from here in this discussion is obviously a product of your own belief structure.)

RAPE: Wyatt, one of the worst things that one person can do to another is to force them to have sex. When a stronger person (usually a man) uses his strength to make a smaller, weaker person (usually a woman) have sex, it turns the most beautiful thing in the world into the ugliest thing in the world. It is called *rape,* and it is a very serious crime for which a person can be put in prison for a long time. A person who is raped feels *violated* and used. Very few men are cruel and insensitive enough to try something so awful. If you were around someone like this, you'd probably feel a little strangeness or weirdness about the person, and that would be your warning to stay away.

ABUSE: Rape is the worst kind of *abuse,* of course, but sometimes people do other things, such as touching someone's private parts or saying rude or crude things to people or forcing them to do things they don't want to do. Again, very few people are cruel enough or sick enough to do this, so don't be worried about it. But, again, if someone ever touches you in a way that doesn't seem right or tries to get you to do something that seems weird or wrong, get away from that person as quickly as you can and tell me about it right away!

Remember that almost all people love children and would never do anything wrong to them. You'll probably never meet anyone who tries to hurt you or make you do something weird. If anyone ever tries to force you to do anything and keeps you from running away, scream your head off! Everybody around you will want to help you, and you'll totally scare anyone who is trying to harm you.

(Repeat over and over that 999 out of 1,000 people would help a child and never hurt one. Explain that you are having this discussion so your child will know what the word means, not because it's likely to happen. Be sure your child doesn't end the discussion feeling worried or scared. *Note: Starting on page 98 you will find an expanded dialogue for warning your child about abuse.*)

PROSTITUTION: Another very sad thing about sex that happens with some people is called *prostitution.* Prostitutes are people who sell their body. They accept money from another person to have sex with that person. It's like the fake marriage roses that people were buying in the fable I read to you [page 43]. Remember how they got all ugly and made people sick? Prostitution is another way to make the most beautiful thing into the most ugly thing. We shouldn't judge people who are prostitutes—maybe their life has been hard or ugly or maybe they need money desperately or maybe they were abused themselves in some way. We shouldn't judge them, but we should feel sorry for them and for those who pay money to have sex with them because they are turning a beautiful thing into a sad and ugly thing. Another not as good word for a prostitute that you may hear is "whore."

MASTURBATION: As boys and girls go into puberty their sex organs (the boy's penis and the girl's clitoris above her vagina, just inside her vulva) become mature and can have an erection, which means blood flows into them and they get larger. *Erections* can be caused by rubbing the penis or clitoris. This can feel very pleasant and can lead to a *climax* (the "lovely shudder" we read about when you were eight that happens when a man and woman have sex.) When someone rubs himself or herself and causes a climax, it is called *masturbation*. With a boy, semen (the fluid containing sperm) comes out of the penis during masturbation. Sometimes boys and girls have dreams about sex and have erections or sexual feelings while dreaming. With a boy, semen may come out during the dream, so it is sometimes called a *wet dream*.

HOMOSEXUALITY: As you know, most boys as they become men are sexually attracted to girls who are becoming women. Girls are usually sexually attracted to boys as they grow up. Men want to marry and have sex with women, and vice versa. That's how babies are made, how families are made, and how the human race keeps going. Households are set up where kids can grow up and receive love and learning so they can get married and have children and families of their own. Some people, though, for reasons we don't fully understand, feel sexually attracted to someone of their own sex. A boy wants to be intimate with a boy, or a girl with a girl. A person who feels this way and has some kind of sex with someone of his own gender is called a *homosexual* or a *gay* person. A gay woman is sometimes called a *lesbian*. Again, we shouldn't judge a person who is gay, but it can be a sad situation because it doesn't allow for the birth of children or for the kind of family that a *heterosexual* couple can have.

AIDS: Some diseases can be passed from one person to another through sex. The worst of these sexually transmitted diseases is called AIDS, which often causes people to die. To protect themselves, people wear condoms to try to keep diseases like AIDS from going from one person to another. They call this *safe* sex, but the best protection is to *save* the most beautiful, awesome thing in the world for one special person.

PORNOGRAPHY: Sometimes people take pictures of the parts of our bodies that we should keep private and modest. Then they put these pictures in magazines or even in videos or on the Internet, and it is called *pornography*. The problem with pornography is that it makes people think too much about sex and think about it in the wrong ways, instead of remembering that it is wonderful and awesome and should be private and personal.

Let your child keep the definition list and notes you have made together if he wants to. Close the discussion positively by returning to the positive notion of how beautiful and awesome sex is when it happens between two people who love each other and are committed and loyal to each other.

Expanded Discussion and Warning About Abuse

Thinking about our children being harmed by sexual predators makes most parents feel physically ill. It's hard to even think about, let alone talk about. Yet it is estimated that one in every three girls is sexually abused in some way during her lifetime (with abuse broadly defined to include everything from verbal abuse and casual touching to rape). Abuse of boys is also shockingly common.

We must warn our children without scaring them. Saying nothing because we hope nothing will happen is probably the worst scenario. But the next worst scenario is saying too much. Making our fun-loving, free-spirited young children feel unsafe and untrusting, regarding everyone as possible offenders, hampers their freedom and takes away their childhood and their innocence.

Every parent has to decide how much warning their child needs and exactly how to present the concepts that follow, but they should not be ignored. Depending on your lifestyle and location, on where you live and your assessment of your child's exposure to danger, you may want to have this discussion before age eight. In many cases it can follow the preemptive discussions just outlined. Much of what is suggested here comes from a friend who is a member of the clinical staff of a very successful youth treatment program and works daily with young women whose lives have become dysfunctional. Though most have problems with drugs and alcohol and sexual acting out, our friend says that the root of almost every problem is the feeling of worthlessness that follows a traumatic experience with sexual abuse. Over 90 percent of her patients have been sexually abused.

DIALOGUE

Natalie, let's talk a little more about abuse. (Review the earlier discussion from this section if you have not recently covered it.) As we were saying, there are a few grown-ups who are very sick in their minds when it comes to sex. Most of them have had bad experiences themselves and don't understand how special and even sacred our bodies are. They have strong urges to do and say things that are not right or proper, sometimes even to children. Although we hope you never meet one of these people, I want you to know exactly what to say and do just in case anything happens that scares or confuses you. Do you think that's a good idea?

Natalie agrees and may ask questions.

First, if a person says crude sexual things to you or tries to touch you in a bad way or on your private parts, he knows that what he is doing is wrong, and he will probably tell you not to tell your parents. This is your clue to do the very opposite. Come and tell me immediately! Even if someone says he will do something bad to someone in your family if you say anything, don't keep secrets. Come and tell me immediately, okay? Promise?

Natalie: Okay.

Has anything like that ever happened to you?

(The answer will probably be negative, but if you sense any hesitation or doubt, probe in a reassuring way.)

Okay, let's do a little role-playing. There are things that will probably never happen, but if they did, you'd know exactly what to do. Pretend I am a person you do not know, and I'm sitting next to you in a movie. Suddenly I quietly reach over and start rubbing your knee. What kind of touch would that be?

Natalie: A bad touch.

Exactly—a bad touch, as we've talked about before. And this is what you should do: Yell very loudly, even if it's embarrassing, "PLEASE DON'T TOUCH ME!" That would be just the opposite of what this strange person expects, and he would leave you alone immediately.

(Actually have your child practice this in a role-play situation. Have her practice her "loud voice" so it will seem more comfortable and logical if the need ever arises. Perpetrators think children are helpless and totally gullible, and this element of surprise will usually stop inappropriate behavior immediately. The attacker is looking for vulnerability and usually chooses quiet or shy victims. If a perpetrator sees anything assertive in a potential victim's behavior, he will usually look for another victim.

Role-play other situations, such as someone rubbing up against her when she is standing in a line. (Have her again practice saying loudly, "PLEASE DON'T TOUCH ME!" until she feels comfortable with it. It's also a good idea to have your child practice screaming. Once she knows how it feels to scream at the top of her lungs, it will be easier to "let loose" if it ever becomes necessary.)

Natalie, you really sounded as if you meant that! Good! There are all kinds of things that people who have bad ideas about sex might do to get you to do what they want. What would you say if someone pulled up in a car beside where you were walking home from school and asked you to help him find his lost puppy or told you to come and get some candy that he has in his car?

Natalie: I'd say, "No way," and I'd get away from there.

Always remember that if someone is trying to harm you, the best thing you can do is make a lot of noise and get away as fast as possible! It's also important not to walk long distances anywhere alone. Do you feel okay about that?

Response.

This same kind of person might also make phone calls to random houses and say scary or nasty things when someone picks up the phone. If that happens to you, what would you do?

Natalie [help and clues]: Hang up without saying a single word, and if the person calls right back, don't answer the phone.

Has anything like that ever happened to you?

Response.

Natalie, the best way to know whether something a person is saying or doing to you is wrong or dangerous is by how it makes you *feel*. If you feel uncomfortable in any way, no matter who is involved—even if it is a family member or a friend or a neighbor—it is extremely important to come and tell me about it. You have a really good thing inside you called a conscience that tells you what is right and what is wrong. Pay attention to your feelings and act on them! If anything an adult says or does doesn't feel right, tell someone! Do you think you can do that?

Response.

As you finish this type of dialogue, reaffirm how much you love your child and tell her that the whole reason for this discussion is that you don't want anything bad to ever happen to her. Reassure her again that almost all adults love children and would always help them and never hurt them. Explain that knowing this stuff is like wearing a seat belt: You probably won't be in an accident, but if you are, you're protected. You'll probably never have one of these abusive experiences, but if you do, you'll know how to protect yourself.

If you do find during this dialogue that your child has had any kind of sexually abusive experience, be very careful in your response. Though you may be feeling intense anger at the perpetrator, be sure your comments are calm, sympathetic, loving, and comforting. Your child will undoubtedly have taken some or all of the blame already. Make sure he or she knows she did nothing wrong! A positive, calm response will have an enormous effect on your child's recovery!

A final note: When I (Linda) was a child, I was pressed sexually by a relative who would visit us once in a while. I felt very uncomfortable from the time he entered my house until he left. I knew enough to stay as far away as possible, but discussing it with my parents was the furthest thing from my mind. I think if I had been asked point-blank if there were any uncomfortable sexual situations in my life, I could have talked about it. I'm sure my parents, who are now both deceased, had no idea there was ever a problem and would have been astonished if I had told them. I carried a big burden and worry in my mind until I became an adult and was able to sort out what had transpired. Making our children aware of dangers and talking to them about things that may already have made them feel uncomfortable is one of the greatest services we can offer them.

Outside of the circle of family and friends, there are predators who can do great damage to our children. One year an inmate in the state prison got our name from a newspaper article about our writing and family activities. Somehow he got our address and started writing to us. He explained that he had no living relatives of his own and was lonely and needed some friends. He explained that he particularly loved children and that it would mean a lot to him to hear from our children. He explained that he had written some bad checks and was paying dearly for it. We felt compassion for this man whose life seemed so stark without family or friends. Our children began drawing pictures for him and sending delightful letters to him. It was good for them to feel they were helping someone in need of a family, and we knew he would be delighted with their childlike love. After a few letters back and forth, we were delighted that he was a nice person and was obviously sorry for what he had done. We hoped he would have a chance to start a new life once he was released.

When his time to go free approached, he was excited, of course, and said he couldn't wait to meet us. Finally his release date came, and we arranged to meet him in a restaurant downtown. A few days before the exciting event, Richard made a few calls to get details on his convictions. You have probably already guessed that this man's conviction was for child molestation. Needless to say, our children never met him. But Richard and I had lunch with him. He came clean and talked about his hangups. Honestly believing that he had finished a bad chapter in his life, he talked freely about his life as a child molester. He confided that he had waited in rest rooms at movie theaters and sometimes in grocery stores for unsuspecting children. Details of his sad and sordid life poured out. Obviously repentant, he explained that he genuinely loved children—too much! Although I felt sorry for him, I left this meeting feeling physically ill. We never saw or heard from him again, but he taught me a great lesson that day about my own gullibility and vulnerability.

How can we protect our families from these misguided individuals who ruin the lives of innocent children? How can we protect them from the unrepentant, skilled perpetrators? No criminal is scarier or more addicted than a bona fide pedophile. And, unfortunately, there is no foolproof way to ensure that our children are never exposed to them. The best insurance is to walk that fine line of warning without worrying, preparing without preaching, and talking without terrifying. Child abuse is so rampant that we have a huge responsibility to protect our children by making them aware of ways to protect themselves.

One added note: Child psychiatrists tell us that the next worse thing to child abuse is parents who don't handle the news that their child—or, more often, teenager—has been abused. The most common response, especially to a teenager's confession, is "You are so stupid! Why were you there? Were you drinking or doing drugs? What could have been in your mind to have gotten yourself into that situation?" Parents only make things worse then they make the child feel guilty and heap even more shame on the child. What abused children need to understand is the very opposite of what they are totally convinced of: that it is not their fault! Victims of child abuse are *never* at fault.

Especially for Boys

While most information and discussion about sex are needed equally by and are appropriate for boys and girls, some information is particularly germane to boys, while some is especially important for girls. The suggestions in this section are best delivered by a dad to a son or by another trusted and respected male to a boy. Still, a single mother can adapt this discussion for successful use with her son.

The sample dialogue is presented here as four questions that can be discussed all at once or in two or more shorter parts. The goals are to answer and anticipate questions to keep communication open and trust high; to protect a boy from mistakes that could hurt him and others; to help him develop respect for women and to become a gentle man as well as a gentleman; and to help him begin to think about a marriage built around equality, support, and giving.

Again, the timing of this discussion or discussions should be based on your son's maturity, interest, and curiosity level— sometime between ages eight and twelve.

Common Questions

DIALOGUE

Billy, I'm going to talk to you about some questions that boys your age sometimes have. You've probably heard some of them, and maybe you've wondered about them yourself. We'll answer them together, and if you have other questions as we go along, you can ask them, too, okay? (Pose each question and see what kind of answer or partial answer your child gives. Praise any ideas he has and then help finish each answer.)

COMMON QUESTION 1: Why are some boys much stronger than others, are getting hair under their arms and on their chests and in the pubic area, and are even shaving?

Puberty starts as early as eleven with some boys and as late as fifteen or sixteen with others. There are some advantages to starting early and some advantages to starting late. And even after puberty, some boys have more hair and more beard than others, just as some are taller or shorter. Every person is unique. No two are the same. That's what is wonderful about life!

COMMON QUESTION 2: Why are some penises so much bigger than others?

The same reasons—everyone is unique. Boys who have gone into puberty will have penises and testicles two or three times as big as boys who haven't started puberty yet. When they are all through puberty, their penises will be closer to the same size, but some will be a little bigger and some a little smaller. The size doesn't matter at all. Having a bigger penis doesn't make a person more of a man or stronger or better at sex.

(Note on questions 3 and 4: There are advantages to talking about wet dreams and masturbation before they start happening or at least early, close to the time of onset.)

COMMON QUESTION 3: Are wet dreams bad?

No, they are perfectly natural. When testicles produce sperm, they need a way to get rid of the extra when they get full. Wet dreams do that. And the dreams themselves, about girls or sex or being naked or even about doing things you'd never do in real life, are perfectly fine. They're just dreams, and every normal boy has them.

COMMON QUESTION 4: Is masturbation bad?

The difference between wet dreams and masturbation is that you can have some control over masturbation. Everyone at least experiments with it. But it can be a problem if it becomes a habit or happens too often. It's like diluting something (use an example like putting too much water in the orange juice). If you use sex too much in a way that isn't the best, it could get a little less unique or less exciting, and not as strong or as special as if it were saved for the best time.

Don't try to stop yourself from thinking about sex because you can't. But when sex comes into your mind, think about how beautiful and awesome it can be with the beautiful and special wife you'll have someday. Think about sex happening in the best way, with someone you totally love and totally know. If you try to do this, you won't feel like masturbating as often, and when you do, at least you'll be thinking about the best kind of sex that will happen someday with your wife. Thinking this way will help you want to save yourself for her!

What It Means to Be a Gentle Man

DIALOGUE

Billy, what do you think it means to be a gentleman?

Billy: To be polite, to have good manners.

Good, and it might mean something else, too. Separate the word into its two parts. What would it mean to be a gentle man?

Billy: To be kind, to be nice, not to hurt people.

Exactly right. It's so important to be kind and nice and gentle to everyone. What would be the opposite of a gentle man?

Billy: Someone who is mean and rough and hurts people or hurts their feelings.

Sometimes movies and TV show these macho guys who beat people up or smash cars or yell and scream at people, but you know that's not how most good guys are in the real world, don't you?

Billy: Yes.

Now, Billy, who is usually the biggest and the strongest, men or women?

Billy: Men.

Since they're usually bigger, does that mean men are better than women or should boss them around?

Billy: No.

Of course not. That would be ridiculous because men and women are equal, aren't they? Neither is one tiny bit better than the other, right?

Billy: Right.

Okay, Billy. And what do we call someone who beats up or is rude or mean to a smaller person?

Billy: A bully or a jerk.

Yes. And what would you call a man who acted that way toward a woman or a husband who acted that way toward his wife?

Billy: The worst kind of bully.

Right, and sometimes it's even called marital abuse or spouse abuse. Why would some men act like that?

Billy: They're stupid.

Yes, or maybe they're insecure or depressed or discouraged or just have to try to prove they're stronger than someone or better than someone else in some way. Or maybe that's how they saw their dad treat their mom.

Billy, every human being you ever meet, male or female, will be better than you in some ways and worse than you in some ways. But every human being is equal. Every man, woman, and child deserves your respect and kindness. Nothing makes me prouder of you than when you are a gentleman and a gentle man. (Note: Right after this talk, watch especially for anything your son does that is polite or gentle, and give him lots of praise.)

Avoiding Sexism, Disrespect, and Conquests

DIALOGUE

Pete, let's talk a little more about respect and sensitivity and being a gentleman. When you hear a dirty story or when you hear boys talking about girls as though they were just something to have sex with, are they being cool?

Pete: No, just the opposite. They're being stupid.

When boys talk about the size of a girl's breasts or her bottom or talk about sexual things they'd like to do to a girl, are they showing respect?

Pete [help and clues]: No, they're thinking of her as an object and not as a person. They are thinking like animals and not like real men.

What can you do if thoughts like that come into your mind?

Pete [help and clues]: I can just remind myself that girls are totally equal to boys and deserve respect and real friendship. And I can remind myself again that sex at the right time with someone I totally love is the most beautiful, awesome thing in the world and is worth waiting for.

When you're old enough to date, why do you think you'll want to go out with girls?

Pete: To have a good time, to get to know them, to enjoy their company, and so we can learn from each other.

What about a boy who takes a girl on a date to see how far he can get with her on sex, how much he can kiss her or how much he can touch her?

Pete [help and clues]: He's thinking of her as an object and not as a person—no respect, no sensitivity, the opposite of a gentleman.

How about a guy who brags to his friends about what he did with a girl or how far he got with her?

Pete: Totally stupid. He's just showing that he doesn't have a clue about respect or about equality or about being a gentleman.

What should you do if you hear guys talking this way?

Pete [help and clues]: Just ignore it. Or if it's a good friend of mine, watch for an opportunity when we're alone to tell him that he's my friend and I like him but what he's doing is not cool at all!

Especially for Girls

We take a slightly different approach on topics particularly important to eight- to twelve-year-old girls. Beyond the straight dialogues used for boys, it is important to understand the social and cultural dynamics that have a powerful effect on preadolescent girls in our society.

Like it or not, what preadolescent and adolescent girls need most is to know how to protect themselves—not only from predators and from peer pressure to engage in early and dangerous sex, but from societal and cultural norms that try to force them to grow up too soon, to look and act in certain ways, and to judge themselves too much on their appearance.

We'll deal first with some common questions, as we did with boys, but then we'll move to some thinking about protection and about preserving the individuality, spontaneity, and confidence that too many eight- to twelve-year-old girls begin to lose.

Common Questions

DIALOGUE

Crystal, growing up is such a great thing. It's like the most exciting adventure in the world because so many new things happen. Like any adventure, some parts seem scary or are a bit hard to understand. Have you had any questions since we talked last about puberty, about your body, or about anything else that has come up?

Response.

You know, Crystal, sometimes answers can come before questions. There are a few things that girls often ask and wonder about—maybe when they're just a little older than you are. Why don't we talk about these questions now, and then you'll have the answers when you need them, okay?

Crystal: Okay.

I'll tell you the common questions one at a time. You see how much of an answer you can give, and then we'll talk about each one together for a minute.

(With each question, just talk together, drawing her in as much as possible, until you've covered the main points.)

COMMON QUESTION 1: Why do some girls develop so much faster than others?

Puberty starts as early as nine or ten with some girls and as late as fourteen or fifteen with others. It's nothing to worry about either way. We each have our own unique body, and its timing and size and shape are different from any other body. The smart thing to do is enjoy the changes and be happy with the results. It's exciting to see who we'll become. Everyone has things about their body they like and things they wish were different. But it's neat to be you and to know that there's no one else exactly like you!

COMMON QUESTION 2: When will I get my period, that is, when will I start menstruation?

The onset of menstruation can vary a lot—anytime between eleven and sixteen. About six months or so before your first period you'll probably notice some light yellow stuff, called a discharge, on your underwear. This means things are getting ready to start. And when your periods do start, they're likely to be pretty irregular for a while—even for a few years. You could have one a month for two or three months and then go for two months without one. They will eventually get regular and almost always come about once a month.

COMMON QUESTION 3: How sick do you get with your period?

You're not really sick, but you can feel sick. Sometimes you'll get cramps, which is an uncomfortable achy feeling when you start your period, but medication can help you feel better in a hurry. PMS (premenstrual syndrome) is the term used to describe feelings that may come just before you start your period. It can make you feel depressed, angry, agitated, weird, klutzy, and moody. It can also make you crave certain foods. Some level of PMS is perfectly normal, and it passes quickly.

(Note: This would be a great time for you to share the experiences of your first period if you haven't already. Your daughter will more likely be excited to share hers when the time comes.)

COMMON QUESTION 4: When will I get my breasts, and how big will they be?

Sorry to keep giving the same kind of answer, but it's different for each girl. It takes nearly five years for breasts to fully develop. Here's the sequence: First you'll notice that your nipples get bigger. You'll get "breast buds," which will probably be kind of pointy and a little lumpy at first. You'll start noticing more body odor and start using deodorant. Your hips will get wider, and you'll see some straight pubic hair. You'll start getting armpit hair. Your nipples will get darker in color. Your breasts will continue to develop through all this, and three years or so after you noticed "breast buds," about the time that your pubic hair forms a full triangle, your breasts will be pretty much completely developed.

COMMON QUESTION 5: My vagina is changing and looking weird. Is that normal?

Yes. Vaginas have two sets of "lips," or "labia." The inner set is often quite wrinkly with little bumps and is a brownish pink color.

COMMON QUESTION 6: What about zits, odors during menstruation, stretch marks, and sexual fantasies or thoughts?

First of all, they are all normal. Use medication on pimples and try not to touch or pick them. You may notice odor during your period, but if you change your pad often, other people won't be able to smell it. (Discussion about pads and tampons are usually carried out during maturation programs at school. This may be a good time to discuss this in detail.) Stretch marks may show up on your skin where you grew fast. They will fade as you get older.

Sex thoughts and fantasies are part of puberty and growing up for girls and for boys.

COMMON QUESTION 7: Why am I getting *fat?*

You're probably not. Girls sometimes think they are getting fat when they are really just going through the normal changes of puberty. Sometimes magazines and TV make girls think they should look a certain way, really skinny and sleek. (See the "Ophelia" discussion below.) Sometimes girls get so worried about being fat that they get anorexia, where they don't eat enough and become really skinny and unhealthy, or bulimia, where they make themselves throw up after they eat. Anorexia and bulimia are very serious illnesses. The thing to remember is that the best way to look good and feel good is to keep yourself healthy. You do this by eating good food and getting rest and exercise.

Avoiding the Ophelia Syndrome

The best-selling book *Reviving Ophelia* by Mary Pipher has been a wake-up call for hundreds of thousands of parents of young girls all over America and perhaps the world. In story after story Pipher describes teenage and preadolescent girls who have grown up too fast, whose lives are in turmoil, who have lived with agonizing guilt and depression. Again and again she refers to young, happy-go-lucky, unselfconscious ten- and eleven-year-olds, with creative minds, interested in everything from sports to nature, able to act adaptively in any situation regardless of gender role constraints without worrying if their behavior is considered feminine or masculine. Then, as a result of media and cultural influences, many of these girls shrink into bundles of self-occupied adolescence, preoccupied with how they look and how they are perceived—and, most especially, with how they can please.

The book's title comes from a character in Shakespeare's *Hamlet* who, as a young woman, becomes obsessed with the desire to please. She is controlled by those who are trying to mold her into the kind of person Hamlet would marry. She becomes a pawn, controlled by people who are using her to reach their own ends. In her book, Pipher attributes the problems of many adolescent girls to this same need to please and to feel accepted. The sexy, glitzy portrayal of a "desirable woman" in magazines, TV, and movies becomes the model for what young girls think they should be and what it takes to please others. In trying to jump from being a child to fitting this new, impossible image, young adolescent girls lose much of their individuality and spontaneity as well as their innocence. Many also actually lose twenty or thirty points of their I.Q.

As soon as we read *Reviving Ophelia,* we began talking about what we call the Ophelia Complex with our daughter Charity. She was ten at the time, on the verge of the dangers that Pipher describes. The heart of our talk went something like this:

DIALOGUE

You know, Charity, some girls your age will start worrying a whole lot about what they look like. They will see pictures of beautiful people in magazines, on TV, and in the movies whom they think they would like to look like. They will see high school girls who are beautiful and seem to be having so much fun. They will get the idea that looking "sexy" is more important than anything else in their lives. Do you know what that means?

Charity: I think so.

Do you see this kind of thing happening with any of your friends? (Charity mentioned two friends who didn't want to "play" anymore and who were wearing makeup and trying to be more grown-up than they really were.)

In a way it's really sad when kids want to grow up too fast! Think about that for a minute. You're ten now. How much longer do you get to be a kid?

Charity: Just a few years at the most.

Exactly. You're going to have to grow up soon enough. Is there any need to rush it?

Charity: No, I don't want to grow up too soon.

And you shouldn't! Childhood is a great privilege, and it's also a lot of fun. Sometimes I wish I could be a child again because I had so much fun, and I didn't really realize it would happen only once and then I would never be a child again.

(Then we really went into the Ophelia idea with Charity. She was genuinely fascinated and a little worried—enough to assure us and herself that she did not want it to happen to her or to any of her friends. Since then it has been a marvelously open topic. When we notice someone trying too hard to grow up too soon, Charity points it out and says, "Uh-oh, look out, Ophelia," or when we see Charity showing any "symptoms," we say, "What's up, Ophelia?" She is always quick to reassure us that she's still a kid who wants to stay a kid for a good while longer.)

Predators: Who They Are and How to Avoid Them.

We thought at one time that "predators" was a good word to use with kids. By telling them the meaning of the word in the animal world—an animal that preys on the young and weak—we thought that protection could be enhanced.

We've since become convinced that the positive, "beautiful and awesome" approach to sex is more powerful and motivational with children. We're therefore extremely cautious about introducing any more fear than is absolutely necessary. A dialogue like the following can be helpful without being overly frightening.

We're dealing here with a type of predator that is less sinister and less calculating than the pedophile and the abusers discussed earlier. These more common predators, who certainly wouldn't think of themselves as such, are older boys and men who date and manipulate younger girls.

Well over half of teen pregnancy is caused by a male four or more years older than the pregnant teen. The simple truth is that helping and encouraging our daughters to put off dating until their mid-teen years and then to date boys close to their own age is the most effective thing we can do to help them avoid trouble.

DIALOGUE

Amanda, how old do you think you want to be when you get married?

Response.

The average age of marriage for girls who go to college is about twenty-four or twenty-five. You are eleven, so how many years do you have to go?

Amanda: Thirteen or fourteen.

That's a long time, Amanda. Even when you're fifteen, you'll still have nine or ten years. Do you think there's any big hurry to start dating?

Amanda: Not really.

I don't, either. Do you think some girls start dating too soon?

Response.

(Most girls under twelve don't feel particularly anxious to date, so they are likely to agree.)

What could be some problems with dating too soon?

Amanda [help and clues]: It's a little uncomfortable to be alone with a boy for a whole evening when you're young. You might feel a little embarrassed, and you might miss out on a lot of fun with your friends or with group-type things. You could also get pressured to do sexual things long before you were ready.

Can you still have fun with boys and be friends with boys if you're not dating?

Amanda [help and clues]: Sure. There are birthday parties and group activities and school things.

There are two kinds of dating, as you know. One is group dating, where you're with a boy but it's in a big group and you're never alone. Even on the way there or the way back, you're always at least double-dating because there are at least two couples in the car. The other kind of dating is alone—just you with a boy. What do you think is the best age to start each kind?

(Discuss: Bring out as many reasons as possible for waiting until high school, ninth grade or so, for group dating and for sophomore year or age sixteen for single dating. Point out that kids who wait this long usually have more fun both before and after they start dating. Before they date, they have more time to be with regular friends and don't have the worries of dating. When they do start, they're more socially ready for it, and it is more exciting and meaningful.)

Amanda, one more thing: When you start dating, what age of boys do you think it's best to date?

Amanda: I don't know. My own age, I guess—or older.

Okay, here's an interesting fact and something to watch out for in the next few years and maybe even to warn your friends about. Most teenage girls who get pregnant or who get talked into having sex too soon are with much older boys—four years older or more. What does that tell you?

Amanda: Don't go out with boys who are a lot older than you.

Exactly. It's not as much fun anyway. Stick with boys your own age or maybe a year or two older. Hey, you're only eleven, you don't need to do much thinking about dating yet. But it's not a bad idea to start thinking about when it's best to start and about the type of boys and the age of boys you'll want to date someday.

"I've Been There": A Brief Precedent-Setting Discussion

The single thing that will most encourage your child to be open and communicative with you regarding sex is his conviction that you not only understand, but that you have "been there." It can be hard for children to realize or even imagine that you were once their age, going through similar experiences and feelings. But they love to think about it, and they are fascinated by any stories you can tell them about yourself at their age.

Such stories accomplish at least five important things:

1. They reassure children that they are normal and that what is happening to them happens to everyone.

2. They show your trust in them and encourage their trust in you.

3. They make your child more aware that you can really understand and empathize, and that you won't judge.

4. They encourage your children to share their feelings and experiences with you.

5. They set a precedent that allows you to share your experiences regarding dating in the years ahead when your children begin dating.

The time to relate an "I've been there" incident is usually when your child tells you or hints at something that has happened to him that reminds you of something you experienced. Don't tell an experience that goes well beyond what has happened to your child; it might encourage the child to also go beyond—made bolder by your experience. Try to think of something that is similar to what your child has told you or what your hunch tells you happened to him or her.

DIALOGUES

(You become aware of some kind of curiosity or "game encounter" that your son had with a girl when he was six or seven years old.)

David, you might have had something happen to you that is much like something I remember happening to me. I was at a family reunion once—I was six years old, I think, or maybe seven. One of my cousins was there, a girl in my same grade but from a different town, so I didn't see her very often. We were playing games like tag and stuff, and then she said, "Let's play doctor." First I was the doctor and she took her clothes off, and then she was the doctor and I took my clothes off. I think we were just curious about what each other's bodies looked like. A lot of little kids do things like that, and it's no big deal.

(Your daughter has had an embarrassing experience with bleeding or spotting during one of her early periods.)

Cindy, I remember so well one day at school when I was just about your age. I'd had a couple of periods, but they weren't very regular or predictable yet so I didn't know when to wear a pad. One day I was sitting in school, and I felt something. I was sure the whole seat of my jeans was going to be red with blood. I tied my sweater around my waist, and as soon as recess came, I took off and walked the whole mile back home. It turned out to be just a little blood and probably no one could have seen it, but I was *so* embarrassed.

"I've been there" discussions are obviously best between father and son and between mother and daughter, but a single mom can have a modified version with a son, as can a father with a daughter: I heard of a boy who . . . and so forth.

Remember that the purpose of "I've been there" discussions is to reassure your child that he or she is normal and that you understand. It also puts you in a position to teach or give advice, emphasize your similarities, and recommit to openness, as in the following examples:

You know, David, the next summer when I saw my cousin, she'd grown up a lot, and I think I had, too, so we just didn't do the "doctor" thing again. I think we both realized that we'd just been curious and that we didn't need that kind of game anymore. That's probably how it will be with you, too, now that you're getting older and know so much about what sex is for and how awesome and beautiful it is.

Cindy, isn't it interesting how much the same we are. I had been worried about exactly the same thing that you were. We're so much alike. But I think just about every girl has a similar experience when she's trying to get used to having periods. I like to hear what you're thinking and what's happening to you. It reminds me so much of me when I was your age. Keep on telling me stuff like this, won't you?

Boy Friends and Girl Friends, as Opposed to Boyfriends and Girlfriends

For many "middle-aged" children, prepuberty is a time of some confusion when it comes to relationships with the opposite sex and to the question of boyfriends and girlfriends. On one hand, they are not really that interested yet, but on the other hand, the peer pressure and the "cultural norm" tells them they ought to be "going with someone" (which means being "matched up" with someone more than it means actually going out). They get asked, "Who are you going with?" or "Who do you like?" or "Who is your girlfriend?" And they need to have some kind of an answer. There's nothing harmful in this rather playful matching up except that it may accelerate the real thing. A talk or two like the one that follows can help reduce the pressure that kids feel and give them license to be a child a bit longer. It can also be instrumental in pushing back the advent of serious dating and may even help to retard the premature social growth that puts kids at greater risk.

DIALOGUE

Sometimes kids say they're "going with" someone or that they like her, but what is real dating?

Jared [help, clues]: To actually go somewhere with a girl, to a movie or a party or something.

Exactly. I know lots of kids your age like to say they are going with someone or have a girlfriend, and that's okay, but why do you think real dating ought to come later—say at fifteen or sixteen?

Jared [help, clues]: Then you're old enough to enjoy it and to be safe—and to drive a car to get there.

Good. Jared, is there a difference between a girlfriend and a girl *friend*?

Jared: Yes, a girl friend *is just a friend who is a girl.*

Exactly. Is it all right for a guy your age to have as many girl *friends* as he wants?

Jared: Yes.

Sure it is. And in the next few years, you'll have a lot of boy *friends* and girl *friends*. You'll go to games and parties and have all kinds of fun, and you can save the girlfriends for a little later. Do you agree?

Older Than Twelve: Adapting the Dialogues and Discussions for Older Kids

It has already been mentioned that if your child is older than twelve, you will need to modify many of the earlier discussions. Let us now be more specific in that recommendation and give some suggestions to parents with a child between twelve and fifteen.

Present the "age eight" and puberty discussions in the context of a review and a clarifier rather than as teaching or informing. Be honest and forthright in doing so.

DIALOGUE

Lorraine, you know that I'm anything but perfect as a parent. I'm always wishing I'd done things better, but I want you to know I'm trying because I love you totally! One thing I wish I'd done a better job of is teaching you more about sex while you were smaller. You've learned more about sex from school, from friends, and from TV, movies, and media than you have from me. That's okay because you're a great kid, and I think you probably understand things pretty well, but I wish you and I had talked more about sex earlier on. I'd like to make up for it in a way by talking about some things with you now. Is that okay?"

Response.

Lorraine, I'll tell you what I'd like to do if it's okay with you. I'd like to tell you some stuff about sex that I wish we'd talked about a few years ago. You'll know a lot of it. It will be kind of a review, and it will let me share with you how I feel about some things. Are you up for it?

Response.

You know, Lorraine, I remember when I was your age. I really do, and it wasn't that different from now. I want us to be able to talk to each other about anything, including sexual things. If you'll let me just review some things about sex, a lot of it will be stuff you already know, but you might just learn some new things, too. And it will make us feel closer so you can ask me about things when you need to. Okay?

You can then begin to go through the earlier "age eight" discussion, adjusting the wording to make it more of a review and pausing often to ask, "Did you know that?" or "How much did you know about that?"

Over the following few weeks, go through each of the follow-up discussions as they are shown. Many of them are written for twelve-year-olds and can be adjusted fairly easily for slightly older kids.

Make no mistake: Talking to an older child about sex is harder. It can even be much harder, depending on age, level of existing communication, peer group, and current levels of sexual exposure and sexual activity. *But it is never too late.* The next chapter is for eleven- to sixteen-year-olds. If your child is in this age range, you will need to adapt and cover the previous topics before these discussions can have maximum impact.

A PERSONAL EXPERIENCE THAT BROUGHT IT ALL INTO FOCUS

It was one of those gorgeous autumn days in New York City with slanting yellow sunshine and sparkling blue sky. The perfect day seemed so incongruous with what had just happened. We were standing on the sidewalk on Sixth Avenue, outside the skyscraper offices of one of the world's largest publishers, a publisher we had just walked out on, a publisher most authors would give their eyeteeth to have, a publisher we had just lost.

It was 1988, and we had come to New York to meet with our editors about our book *Teaching Your Children Values,* a treatment of twelve universal values together with methods for parents to use in teaching one value per month to their children. The publishers had paid us a healthy advance on the book and loved the early drafts we had sent them, but we sensed a new mood that day when the senior editor started the meeting with "We like the book but . . . ."

The "but" turned out to be chapter 6, "The Value of Fidelity and Chastity." "We think that chapter should come out," he said. "We want this to be a nineties type of book, and even the words of that chapter title sound old-fashioned."

The meeting went downhill from there. We asked how in good conscience we could write a book on values for families and children—in a time of AIDS and teen pregnancy and the breakdown of families—and not mention sexual morality and behavior. They replied that they didn't want to send parents or kids on a guilt trip. We reminded them that guilt was frequently associated with failure to live in harmony with time-tested values. They argued that there were plenty of "less controversial" values, and therefore there was no need to include one that would polarize people. We suggested that sexual values were what parents needed the most help with. They countered that there were other books for that—books on safe sex and so forth. We offered our view that the vast majority of parents were far more conservative on this issue than the media suggest and that even parents with very liberal and permissive personal sexual attitudes and habits were often quite conservative when it come to how they hoped their children would behave sexually. They misinterpreted that and said they didn't want it to be a political book anyway. Almost in desperation we made the point that readers weren't obligated to teach or implement every value in the book. They could pick and choose. They shook their heads and said they didn't want to force readers to make that kind of choice.

Then they made a mistake—or we did, depending on how you look at it. The senior editor, weary of the debate, raised the stakes by saying, "Well, we're not publishing it unless that chapter comes out." Mumbling something about certain other values that wouldn't allow us to compromise on something so fundamental, we called their bluff and walked out.

Standing in that bright autumn sunshine, we realized what we had done: We had severed a profitable relationship with a huge publisher, a relationship that had taken years to build. Yet, worrisome as it was, it felt right, and the sunshine had some warmth in it after all.

It took us five years and a new agent to hook up with another publisher and release the book in 1993. It shot to the number one position on *The New York Times* best-seller list, the first parenting book to do so in fifty years (since Dr. Spock's *Baby and Child Care*), and, most gratifying of all, we received more comments and thank-you notes from parents on chapter 6 than on any other chapter.

With hindsight, the whole scenario may have been a bit of serendipitous timing. America has been far more values conscious in the '90s than it was in the '80s. In fact, when our book fell from the number one spot, it was replaced by William

J. Bennett's *Book of Virtues.* In the '90s, values and balance and a return to family commitments became buzzwords, and parents not only felt but also acknowledged their need for help.

We feel even more strongly now than we did then that sexual morality along with the ability of children to make wise decisions regarding their sexual conduct is the most relevant value of all with regard to their safety, their physical and emotional health, and their chances for a happy family and a successful life. It is a value that is bombarded and undermined a thousand times a day by the media, which present amoral messages to our children, depicting sex, at worst, as exploitive and violent, and, at best, as something everyone of just about every age does casually, on the first date, without consequences.

We are convinced that the casual sex children see in media is even more dangerous and problematic than the indiscriminate violence. Not many kids go out and copy the violence they see, but countless thousands emulate the casual sex. In doing so they not only endanger themselves but they rob themselves, naively and unknowingly, of the greatest joy, the greatest security, and the most beautiful commitment available in life.

During this whole process, during our ups and downs with the values book, we began to realize how much help parents need not only with combating and overcoming the amoral pull of media and peer group but with the basics—with how to talk to their kids openly and positively about sex, with how to suggest restraint not out of fear or negativism but out of hope in and respect for something gloriously positive: a marriage of commitment and support, and a family with security and love.

The best way to protect our children is not to frighten them, threaten them, or teach them how to have safe sex. The best way is to share with them the spectacular beauty of human intimacy, the awesome wonder of procreation, and the nine-month miracle of the development of a baby—all in a way that is so positive, so reassuring, and so inspiring that it becomes natural to ask them (at many times and in many ways), "Shouldn't something that special be saved for a time of real love, commitment, and safety? Shouldn't it be saved for marriage?"

Friends have asked us, "When did you start writing *How to Talk to Your Child About Sex?*" We answer, "On the sidewalk on Sixth Avenue in 1988."

4

Behavior Discussions with Eleven- to Sixteen-Year-Olds

By the time a child finishes elementary school, the
challenge has completely shifted from teaching him about
sex to teaching him about how to view (and what
to do with) sex. It's a question now of attitude
and behavior rather than knowledge.

Shifting from Basics to Behavior

At this point, assuming that you've had the earlier discussions with your child, the facts he or she needs to know about sex are pretty well in place, and you have established a positive and upbeat attitude about the beauty and wonder of mature, committed sex. The question now is one of actual practice and behavior. In this chapter, with eleven- to sixteen-year-olds in mind, the goal is teaching and encouraging sexual restraint and responsibility.

All parents want to safeguard and protect their children, and as we meet with fellow parents throughout the country, the overwhelming majority feel that abstinence, at least through the high school years, is the best kind of protection to work for and the best safeguard of a happy childhood and a good marriage and family later on.

Although they know what a challenge it is, many parents today hope for a greater degree of sexual restraint in their children than what they practiced themselves. Our children's world is simply more dangerous than the one we grew up in. The stakes are higher now; they have more to lose and more to gain. There is more to worry about, more to protect from, and more need for solid, lasting family commitments. As Leonard Pitt wrote in a Knight Ridder/Tribune News Service article quoted earlier,

> The job of steering children to adulthood has become downright frightening. . . . The price of misstep has never been so high, nor pop culture so determined to trade upon their innocence—and damn the consequences. Which is why it has never been more incumbent upon parents to repeat ignored warnings . . . because one day you must surrender your children to the flood [of sex that pervades our society] and before that happens, you ought to teach them to swim.

Bottom line: It's both harder and more essential for kids in today's world to practice sexual restraint and responsibility. So how can parents teach it and encourage it? The only way we know, other than by example, is through the honest, open communication and reasoning that the dialogues and discussions of this chapter promote.

Parents who read this book fall into one of two groups: those who now have a reasonably strong and loyal marriage, and those who do not. Each group has a separate but powerful motivation for helping their children to avoid high-risk, too-early sex and to strive for a solid, loyal marriages of their own. Parents in the first group are often motivated by a love that hopes their children will have the same kind of commitment and security they feel. Parents in the second group are motivated by a love for their children that wants them to have something they themselves are missing. The second motivation is as strong as the first. In a way the parents of the second group, who succeed in giving their children something beyond what they have, are the real heroes of this world. They are the ones who will change the next generation for the better. And the change often continues for generations, giving grandchildren and great-grandchildren the wonderful gift originally given by the parent who looked for improvement and progress rather than for self-justification and continuation of the same pattern.

Helpful Metaphors

Everyone learns well and remembers well from good metaphors and clear, understandable comparisons—particularly children. The best metaphor we know to teach the beauty of sexual responsibility to young children is "The Marriage Roses," the fable used in the first chapter. We have some other favorites for eleven- to thirteen-year-olds. These can be adapted to use almost like stories, or they can be brought up to spur discussion when you sense a need to reinforce or clarify various aspects of the beauty, the power, and the privacy and importance of sex.

DIALOGUES

HORSE AND BRIDLE

Andy, do you know how much a horse weighs?

Response.

An adult horse weighs over a thousand pounds—at least six times as much as most riders. And how much stronger do you think a horse is than a rider?

Andy: Six times as strong?

At least! Horses are amazingly strong! But when a good rider goes out on a horse, who is in charge of where they go and how fast they go, the horse or the rider?

Andy: The rider.

Well, how come? The horse is much stronger. Why doesn't he just go wherever he wants instead of going where the rider wants him to go?

Andy: Because the rider is smarter?

Well, being smarter helps, but the rider needs something else to be in control of the horse. Do you know what it is?

Andy: A bridle?

Exactly. A bridle is something that has reins for the rider to hold. It goes around the horse's head and has a bit that goes through its mouth, behind its teeth. It doesn't hurt the horse, but just by pulling gently in one direction, the rider can pull the horse's head around and make it turn, or he can pull back on the reins and the horse will stop. By bridling the horse, the rider controls it. Would you like to try to ride a big, strong, spirited horse without a bridle?

Andy: No way!

Why?

Andy: It would be dangerous.

It sure would! The horse could throw you, injure you, even kill you. Horses aren't usually mean, but they are very big and very strong—so much stronger than you. If you don't have a bridle to control them, they're just way too dangerous. But with a bridle they are fantastic. They can take you for beautiful, awesome rides. Galloping on a horse is one of the most thrilling things you can do. So what makes the difference between dangerous and wonderful?

Andy: The bridle.

Exactly. Now here's the big question, Andy. How is sex like a horse?

Andy [clues and help]: Well, it is very strong. The urges and feelings of sex are powerful. And, like a horse, it's beautiful and awesome.

What else?

Andy: It can hurt us and be very dangerous if it's not controlled. It can start a baby, it can make people feel used or abandoned or violated. It can even make people very sick if its power isn't used at the right time in the right way.

Right. And if it is bridled and controlled, sex is thrilling and awesome and not dangerous at all. How do we bridle sex?

Andy: Don't use it until you're married. Marriage is kind of the bridle, isn't it?

Very good. That's exactly right. When people save sex until they are married, sex is not dangerous at all. It's controlled and it's thrilling and it's—

Andy: I know, I know—beautiful and awesome.

Exactly. Our two favorite words about sex, and they work to describe a horse, too.

The Decisions in Advance that you've made are a good bridle for now . . . until you get the bridle of marriage later on.

TEN DOLLARS OR ORLANDO

Ashley, what if someone said to you, "You have two choices. If you want, I will give you ten dollars right now, or if you'll wait until next summer, I'll take you to Disney World in Orlando, Florida." Which one would you choose?

Ashley: Orlando.

Well, of course you would. It's obviously better. But you'd have to wait until summer, and you wouldn't get the ten dollars that you'd like to have right now. Is that okay?

Ashley: Sure. I'd much rather wait and go to Disney World.

Ashley, sex is so much like that. Waiting until you're married makes it so good and so special and so new—like waiting until summer to go to Orlando. Having sex before—with someone you're not sure you truly love—is like taking the ten dollars now. It's a ten-dollar bill, but it doesn't last very long, and as soon as you spend it, you wish you'd waited for something so much better. Does that comparison make sense to you?

Response.

Follow up and review as necessary.

DIAMONDS

Curtis, do you know how diamonds are made?

Curtis: Not really.

Well, diamonds start out as coal, deep in the ground. The pressure of all the rocks and earth on top of them condenses the chunk of coal, pushing it tighter and tighter together, and making it smaller and smaller and harder and harder until, after a couple of million years, it becomes a diamond. So, Curtis, think about it. How much more is a diamond worth than a chunk of coal?

Curtis: A million times as much.

Right. And what did the coal have to do to turn into a diamond?

Curtis: It just had to wait.

Yes, it had to wait. Anything else?

Curtis: It had to have a lot of pressure on it.

That's right, waiting and pressure. Now if someone came along and took the clump of coal out of the mountain before it had the time and the pressure, would it be very beautiful?

Curtis: No, just a black lump.

Would it be worth very much?

Curtis: No. Well, maybe you could burn it and it would keep you warm for a night, but that's about all.

Curtis, is there lots of coal?

Curtis: I think so.

There sure is. It's under the ground in so many places. There are millions of tons of it. How about diamonds? Are there tons of them under the ground, too?

Curtis: No.

Right. Compared to coal, diamonds are much rarer and much, much more beautiful and valuable. Can you guess why we're talking about all this?

Curtis: Another comparison with sex?

Right. It is another metaphor. (Explain the meaning if you haven't before.) What do coal and diamonds represent?

Curtis [help and clues]: Sex, two kinds of sex: the really common, not so pretty kind that no one waits for, and the brilliant, beautiful, and rarer kind that you have to wait for until you're married.

Good. How about the pressure?

Curtis [help and clues]: There's a lot of pressure on people to have sex too early. If you endure that pressure and stand up for what you believe, you'll have a diamond later on.

Very good. Why is it like the coal if you use it too soon?

Curtis: Because if you burn it, it might keep you warm for one night, but then it's gone—and it never turns into a diamond.

FROGS

Jane, this is a weird question. I can't imagine why you'd ever want to, but do you know how to cook a frog?

Jane: No.

Well, it's interesting. If you just toss a frog into boiling water, he's so quick that he just jumps right out the second he feels the heat. But if you put him in a pan of cool water and set it on the stove, the frog gets nice and comfortable, and the water heats up so gradually that he doesn't really notice it. Before long, he is cooked. Weird, huh?

Jane: Yeah, weird.

Well, I bet you've guessed by now. What do you think this is?

Jane: Another metaphor about sex.

Right again. What is the frog?

Jane: Sex, I guess, or having sex too early.

Yes, or maybe that frog is you and the water is sex. Now, say we just took you and some boy and suddenly put you in a room together, both naked. You'd jump out of there as fast as that frog, wouldn't you?

Jane: I sure would.

Why?

Jane: Well, because I'd be embarrassed, and I'd know it wasn't right to be there with him like that.

Right. But what if you were with that boy on a few dates? You start getting really comfortable with him. But then let's say things started warming up a little. He started to want to do more than a little kissing. What would that be like in the metaphor?

Jane: It's getting a little too hot. You need to get out before it boils and you start to cook.

Right on, Jane! You are not a frog, you're smarter. You notice when the water starts getting too hot. You hop out. You save yourself for water that will stay cool and safe. You save yourself until the water can be what?

Jane: I know, I know—until the water can be the most beautiful and awesome thing in the world!

WORLD TRADE CENTER

John, use your imagination for a minute. Let's say we're taking a trip to New York City, and one thing we want to do is go to the top of the World Trade Center, the two tallest buildings in the city, over one hundred stories high. We're going to go up there to the observation deck and look down on the whole city—even see the Statue of Liberty and all the bridges across the rivers. Okay?

John: Okay.

We get maps and pictures of the city, and we really look forward to our trip. When we get there, we don't go to the building right away. We wait for a clear day when there are no clouds and very little smog. The perfect day finally comes. It rained the day before and blew the dirt out of the air, and it's a crystal clear day. You can see forever. Are we excited?

John: We're excited!

We ride up in the fastest elevator in the world. The guy in a uniform who operates the elevator is a little grumpy, but going up in that elevator is like taking off in a rocket. We get up there and take our time walking around the observation deck, looking through telescopes, spotting the landmarks we've seen on our maps in our picture books. It's a great day. Does that sound like fun?

John: Yes.

Good, John. Now, here's the point: Compare yourself and how much you enjoyed that experience in our story with how much another person from our story enjoyed it—the elevator man. Who enjoyed it most, you or the person who ran the elevator?

John: I did.

Why?

John [help and clues]: Because it was new and special to me. He does it every day. It's old stuff to him. He has seen it all before.

Right, plus he didn't look forward to it and prepare for it. Now, how can we compare that with sex?

John [help and clues]: Someone who looks forward to the most beautiful, awesome thing in the world and waits for just the right time and the right person will enjoy it so much more than someone who does it all the time.

Right, John. When you save this beautiful thing called sex, it gets more romantic, more exciting, and more special.

As we try to come up with metaphors, comparisons, and symbols to help our children understand the vast differences between casual and committed sex, we ourselves ought to pause for a minute and reflect on what a powerful symbol sex is. Two becoming one, a uniting, a merging, a mutual gift, joining, connecting, becoming one flesh, synergy (one plus one equals family), or reverse synergy (one plus one equals one). Almost everything couples in love want to have happen to them emotionally, mentally, and spiritually is symbolized by the physical act of sex.

When all these "joinings" are really wanted mentally, emotionally, and spiritually, when we're willing to commit to them, then the symbolic part of physical sex is hugely desirable and enjoyable. When people are tentative and hesitant and unsure about the mental, emotional, and spiritual parts of the relationship, then the physical symbolizes nothing and can sometimes feel like a dishonest act (or at least a very shallow act).

Pornography and Media Images

Eleven- and twelve-year-olds (and those older and younger, too, but especially in this age range) hear all kinds of words and phrases through media, peers, school, and reading that they know (or sense) are connected to sex but that they neither understand nor can correctly define. Some words and phrases come at them innocently from friends and acquaintances, while others present themselves through videos or the Internet or explicit music or off-color jokes or stories that could be disturbing or even threatening.

Unfortunately, no matter how we try to shelter or protect them, our children will see as well as hear a lot of sexually explicit stuff. The pornography that most of today's parents grew up with was almost comically mild compared with what our children are exposed to today. It's probably as easy and as likely for your child to run onto hard-core pornography on the Internet as it was for you to chance on a *Playboy* magazine during your childhood. And your child can find much more sexual content surfing through the standard cable TV channels than you could in movie theaters.

As much as most parents wish we could protect the ears and eyes of our kids, it simply isn't possible. What is possible is to precondition them to a positive view of sex so that they see negative, gross, and dangerous depictions of sex for exactly what they are: deviations from what they know is right and from what they know is best.

With the goal of a positive attitude and with an ongoing commitment to keep the subject open and positive, look for opportunities to have discussions something like the following.

DIALOGUE

Tyson, do you know what I mean when I say that almost everything can have a good side and a bad side?

Tyson: No, not exactly.

Well, take fire for example. If it's used correctly, it heats our houses and our water, cooks our food, and so on. But its bad side is that it can burn down buildings or forests, even kill people. See what I mean? Almost everything is that way. Television is great if we watch good stuff and don't watch it too much. But if you become a couch potato or watch gross stuff, that's the bad side. Understand?

Response.

Now, Tyson, sex is the same way. We've been talking about the light side, the good side, ever since you were eight. And sex can be so good that we always call it what?

Tyson: The most beautiful, awesome thing in the world.

Right on! And it is! But, like everything, it has a dark side if people use it wrongly or talk about it in a gross or ugly way. Do you think you've ever heard or seen anything about sex that was kind of on the wrong side?

Response. Help Tyson think about this, about any words he has heard in songs or from friends that didn't sound beautiful or awesome, or pictures he has seen on TV or on the computer or in magazines that seemed a little weird or a little wrong or that didn't make him feel too good about sex, or crude sexual words he has heard. Don't probe or push, just see what's in his head. *Remind him that the correct words are "sexual intercourse" or "making love."*

It's like what we just said, Tyson. You can twist a good thing around or use it wrongly and make it seem bad or weird or silly instead of special. There are also some words for the private or sexual parts of a boy or a girl that are kind of crude or disrespectful. As we've discussed before, the correct name for your private parts are "penis" and "testicles." Have you heard other names used?

Response. If he has, review them with him. If not, tell him that he will.

It's not that these words are so bad or terrible, they're just not the correct words and are often used in silly ways or to tell jokes or make fun of someone—usually by people who don't know how special and beautiful sex can be.

You'll also remember from our earlier talks that the correct name for a girl's private parts are "vagina" and "breasts." Have you heard other names for these?

Response. Same type of explanation. Don't overdo your criticism of wrong words or make Tyson judgmental of those who use them. Just stress that "those who know" use the right words.

Now, Tyson, sometimes movies and music and TV and magazines and books use the wrong words, too. Can you think of something else that movies or TV or magazines sometimes do that doesn't show respect and doesn't show how special sex is?

Response. Help Tyson with the idea that some pictures show sex or people's private parts in ways that don't show respect or don't make it seem special.

Now let's think about that a little, Tyson. Our bodies are beautiful and awesome, right? Boys' bodies and girls' bodies—every part of them is special and wonderful. And sex is the most beautiful and special thing, right?

Tyson: Yes.

Well, then, why not show pictures of all of our bodies and of people having sex? Why not show it on movies and TV and computers and magazines?

Tyson: Because it's private and special, and it should just be with someone you love. (Reinforce that—or help Tyson come to that conclusion with some of the following analogies: If you had a really special beautiful secret and you told it to everyone or put it on the Internet, would it be a special secret anymore? If you had an extra-special birthday present for your best friend but you gave it to a lot of other people to use for a day before your friend's birthday, would it still be a special birthday present? If there was a movie you really liked and you got it on video and watched it every day, do you think you'd still love it, or would it get a little boring? Let's say you had some really great fireworks for the Fourth of July, but you started lighting a few of them every night or two. When the Fourth of July came, you didn't have any left; would you have a really fun holiday? What if you had a beautiful new car but you drove it in the mud, let it sit out in the snow, and left the keys in it so others could drive it anytime they wanted. Would it stay beautiful for long?) When you feel that Tyson really gets it, go on.

There is actually a word for showing sex in a way that isn't beautiful and awesome and private. Do you know what it is?

Tyson: Pornography.

That's right, and where might you find pornography?

Tyson: In movies, TV, the Internet, and magazines.

And why is it best not to see it?

Tyson: It makes sex not seem so special as it should be.

Is it really bad or terrible if you just happen to see it?

Tyson [clues and help]: No. A lot of times you might see it without even trying to. But you should try not to look for it.

What's the best thing to do if you do see some pornography?

Tyson: Don't keep looking at it.

Good. *And* tell me about it so we can talk about it. That way I can

.help you understand why it was there. By the way, Tyson, why do you think people put pornography on TV, in movies, and in magazines?

Tyson: I don't know.

Well, this is really interesting. They do it to make money. Remember the story about the marriage roses? Some people ruined the marriage roses and sold them to make money. It's the same with pornography. People know that if someone doesn't understand how beautiful and special and private sex should be, they will buy pornography or watch it in a movie or whatever. Do you think it's good to try to make money from sex?

Tyson: No.

It's like the people who sold the marriage roses. When others bought those fake marriage roses, they made themselves sick and made the people who were selling them very rich. When we look at pornography, we make ourselves kind of sick and make the people who produce it rich. So what do you think?

Tyson: We shouldn't do it.

Right, Tyson. You are such fun to talk to about these things. You understand so well, and I like having discussions with you. Remember: Sex is beautiful and fantastic and good, but pornography is bad. It's making something beautiful look cheap. And using the wrong words to talk about sex or about our bodies is a bad idea, too. Let's have a deal. You promise to tell me when you run into pornography or hear words that are disrespectful about sex, and I'll promise to talk with you about it and help you understand. Okay?

Tyson: Okay.

If your child has Internet access at home, you should have some form of censoring software to block pornography. We think the best one currently is *Cyberpatrol*. Two other favorites, available at most computer stores, are *Net Nanny* and *Surf Watch*. Remember that these "blockers" are not the complete answer. They won't block everything that is objection-able, and your child probably won't go online only in your home. The best protection is the kind of dialogue and commu-nication suggested in the foregoing dialogue.

Channeling and Integrating Sexual Thoughts

As children move through puberty, their increasing hor-monal activity will turn their thoughts ever more frequently toward sex. With the "beautiful and awesome" orientation of the preceding parental discussions, they can handle this posi-tively and can welcome rather than resent their puberty.

There are two thought patterns that can help them avoid thinking about sex in ways that are exploitive or negative or troubling. We call one *channeling,* and it involves orienting any sexual stimulation toward the future and toward a vision of a happy marriage and beautiful, committed sex (that is, "I see stuff and get turned on, but it just makes me know how exciting it will be when I find the right person"). We call the other thought pattern *integrating,* which means consciously putting thoughts of sex into the broader context of love (that is, "When I find the person I love enough to marry, I'll have many ways to show my love; one will be through physical sex").

Both of these techniques acknowledge how natural and normal it is for adolescents to think about sex. They let a child accept rather than worry about his sexual thoughts, but they channel and integrate them into a positive context where they actually become reminders of how beautiful and awesome sex can be.

DIALOGUE

Sam, as we discussed before, part of puberty is that you have a lot of thoughts about sex—even at night in your dreams. But during the daytime, too, you'll notice more that has to do with sex and think about it more. I guess you've already noticed that.

Response.

These thoughts are totally normal, Sam. Everybody has them. In fact, you can't *not* have them. It doesn't do any good for someone to tell you not to think about something. That actually makes you think about it more. For example, what if I say to you, "Sam, don't think about a giraffe." What are you thinking about right now?

Sam: A giraffe.

So when something comes into your mind about sex, you can't always kick the thought out, but what you can do is *change* the thought a little if you need to. For example, let's say something comes into your mind that is a little gross—a pornographic picture you saw, perhaps—or maybe you just have a sexual thought about some girl you know. Instead of trying to kick the thought out, which is sometimes impossible, you can change or transform the thought by just thinking about how beautiful and awesome sex will be someday with the person you marry. Just quickly change the thought this way, and then go and do something to get your mind on other things. Does that make sense?

Response.

So, Sam, let's review that. If you're having a lot of thoughts about sex and some are kind of gross or crude—thoughts that aren't very beautiful or awesome—what can you do?

Sam [help and clues]: First, I can change the thought so I'm thinking about the wife I'll someday have and truly love. That will help me think about sex positively, as something beautiful and awesome, something worth waiting for. Also, I can remember that sex is only a good thing if it's part of love.

Sam, that's exactly right. You know, I love you so much, and I love telling you this stuff. Sex really can be the most beautiful and awesome thing, and no matter how others think of it, you can think about it as a way to show real love to a very special person you'll meet someday.

Waiting on Dating

Essentially, most American kids grow up too soon and start dating too early, and most parents, if they could, would prefer to retard the social growth of their kids a bit. The trouble is, an authoritative or dictatorially restrictive approach often causes rebellion and experimentation rather than responsible behavior. A respectful, reasoning approach with a thirteen- or fourteen-year-old—something like the following—usually produces better results.

DIALOGUE

Peter, this might sound like a strange question, but do you feel as if you're completely ready to be an adult right now?

Response.

Would you like to be a full-fledged adult right now?

Response. Peter will probably say "no." If he hesitates, point out some difficult things about adulthood. Help him feel grateful to be young and without all those responsibilities.

Well, let's think for a minute about the whole business of growing up. You're thirteen now. If we decided that adulthood started in a few years—when you are 18, say—and if you lived to be eighty-eight, how long would you be an adult?

Peter: Seventy years.

That's a pretty long time, isn't it? How long do you get to be a child?

Peter: Just a few years.

Exactly. So do you think you should be in a big rush to turn into a grown-up or an adult?

Peter: No, not really.

Of course you want to be grown up in some ways—like being responsible and dependable. But it's great that people get to be a child for a while and then a teenager for a while. And it's important to be a student for a few years before you have a full-time job and to be a grown-up single person for a time before you get married. If you rushed through any of these, what would you be doing?

Peter [help, clues]: I'd be missing out on some things.

Exactly. Peter, what do you think is about the right age to get married?

Peter: Maybe twenty-five or so. (Guide him to the age range you think is best by asking subquestions about college, maturity, and so forth.)

Okay, well, that's twelve years from now. How many years do you think a boy has to be dating girls before he can find the one he wants to marry?

Peter: I don't know. A few years, I guess.

Yeah, I think a few years. If a guy started dating when he was fifteen or sixteen, would he have plenty of time? How much?

Peter: Nine or ten years.

That's plenty of time, isn't it, Peter? What is dating?

Peter: Going out.

Right. Going out one-on-one with a girl, which really works best starting at about age sixteen. Why sixteen?

Peter: Well, you can drive a car then.

True, and that's a lot better than having a parent drive you or walking. Also, dating is just a lot more comfortable when you're sixteen. You're more relaxed and ready for it. Do you think you'd be willing to wait until you're sixteen to start real dating?

Response. Help Peter to see the wisdom and safety in this. Reassure him that you have no problem with group dates or boy-and-girl parties as long as they're organized and have some adult supervision or attendance. Suggest that he have some of that kind of activity in your own home.

How often do you think a sixteen-year-old should single-date?

Peter [help and clues]: Not too often. Maybe a couple of times a month. Not more than once a week. Not so much that it gets in the way of school and other activities.

Dating can be such a great thing, but it can also be expensive. And if it happens too much, it can make you miss out on a lot of group things or other social activities with a lot of other kids. We'll talk more about how often you think you should date.

Here's another question. Once you are sixteen and you start dating, Peter, what do you think is best at first—to go steady with just one girl or to "play the field"?

Peter [help and clues]: Play the field. That way you meet more people, learn more, get better at social interaction, and start figuring out what you do and don't like in a girl.

I agree. Peter. At least for a year or two after you start dating, play the field and don't go steady. If everyone thinks you're going with just one girl, you don't get near as many chances to date or even meet other girls. Do you see my point?

Peter: Yes.

A lot of kids really don't intend to go steady, but it's just easier to keep asking the same girl. It's sort of more comfortable and less risky, so they just end up with one person all the time. How could you avoid that, once you start dating?

Peter: I don't know. Just ask out different people, I guess.

This book I have here suggests an interesting idea. You just decide to never take the same girl out three times in a row. In other words, once you've had two straight dates with a girl, even if you really like her, you have a deal with yourself that you'll take someone else out before you have another date with the first girl. Can you think of any benefits or advantages of that policy?

Peter [help and clues]: It might keep you from getting too involved, and it might cause you to meet and get to know girls you wouldn't have dated otherwise.

Great, Peter! We have a couple of years to think more about the whole dating thing, but it's going to be great, something to really look forward to. In the meantime, keep me posted on what your friends are doing and how you're feeling about social things. I can remember a lot from when I was your age, and it will be fun to talk about what I did then and compare it with what you're doing now.

Dress Rehearsals

In connection with the Decisions in Advance suggested earlier, role-playing and case study–type discussions can serve as dress rehearsals for situations and can greatly increase your child's chances of making good decisions when are under pressure. Good case studies essentially involve putting your child in an imaginary yet realistic situation and having him or her mentally role-play exactly what to say and what actions to take.

This type of discussion is particularly useful as a follow-up or reinforcer of decisions made in advance and is particularly well suited for twelve- to fourteen-year-olds. For example, let's say your nine-year-old has made (and signed and recorded in her journal) a decision in advance not to have sex while in high school. Now she is fourteen and gaining a much more realistic sense of how difficult her decision may be. A discussion such as the following may strengthen her.

DIALOGUES

Jennifer, I know some of your friends are dating, and one or two of your older friends are pretty serious with boyfriends. Are you hearing anything about their sexual involvement?

Response. See how much Jennifer knows and how much she will tell you. Indicate that you know some girls her age are sexually active, and others are trying to decide what they should or shouldn't do.

How are you feeling about your decision in advance to wait?

Jennifer: Fine. I still think it's the right thing to do. (If she is wavering, you may want to review some of the reasons that she made the decision.)

Good. You know that I think that's right, too. Do you think it may be harder than you thought when you first made the decision?

Response.

Well, having gone through the high school years myself, I can tell you that you'll face some pretty tough pressure about it from boys and maybe even from girls. Let's just role-play a couple of things that might happen—kind of like a dress rehearsal. Okay?

Jennifer: I guess.

First, let's say you're with two of your girlfriends. Both of them have had sex, and they're telling your how cool it was. They start saying things like "Come on, Jen. When are you going to join the real world?" and "What's your problem? Do you think you're better than we are?" and "How are you going to know what you're missing if you don't try it even once?" What will you say?

Response. Help Jennifer actually decide on some specific responses that she feels good about: "I just made a decision a while ago to wait, and I feel good about it" or "Look, I'm not judging you. I just think for me it's best to wait." Role-play a dialogue back and forth. Give a lot of praise and reinforcement.

Similar discussions can reinforce earlier decisions in advance about drugs, smoking, drinking, or other topics, most of which are directly related to sexual decisions. Another example is twelve-year-old Robert, who made a decision in advance at age ten not to do drugs, not even once. He's now spending time with a couple of friends that you are a little concerned about.

DIALOGUE:

Robert, I was thinking about your decision in advance not to ever try drugs. That's such a great decision. Do you still feel good about it?

Response. Bolster and reinforce if necessary.

Good, I'm totally proud of you. As you get older, you can get even more specific and strong on that decision. In fact, you can practice it mentally. All you do is imagine a situation where there would be a big-time pressure on you to try something. Then just rehearse in your mind what you would do. I'll help you on one. Close your eyes and try to imagine this:

You're at a party at someone's house, Rob, and you're standing in a little group with some of your friends, just talking. A guy comes over who is a known druggie, and you think maybe he'll start offering marijuana as he has at school, but instead he has some pills. He says, "How about it, guys? You goodygoodies won't do coke or grass, but these little uppers are harmless. You like them, don't you, Jeff and Pete?"

You're surprised because Jeff and Pete are your good buddies, and you thought they felt the way you do about any kind of drugs. But they both take a pill from the guy, and Jeff says, "Yeah, these things are okay, guys. You just feel energized for a while. It's cool." The other three guys in the group take one, too, and all eyes are on you. "Come on, Rob. What's wrong? We've tried these. They're not really drugs. You can get them from the pharmacy." What do you do?

Response. Role-play a dialogue until Robert is comfortable with a good, strong response such as, "Sorry, guys. It's just a promise I made to myself a while back. You don't want me to break a promise, do you?"

Interestingly, I (Richard) had one experience with this type of "scenario thinking" that I'll never forget. I was counseling a young man I really liked and cared about. (I think he was about fifteen at the time.) He had made a decision to wait before having sex, but he seemed too flippant and easy about it. On impulse I had him imagine a situation. I described him alone in a car a year or so later, with a girl he really liked and was really attracted to. I embarrassed him a little by describing how good it felt to kiss her and how she seemed to want him to do more, how it felt to lay on top of her in the car. Then

I had him imagine her hand guiding his under her clothes. I asked him what he'd do.

"Take her home," he said—too quickly, too easily.

"No," I said, "come on. I was specific with you. You tell me in detail what you'd do. Rehearse it."

So, a little exasperated with me, he said, "Okay. I'd sit back up, reach in my pocket, get the car keys out, and turn on and start the car. I'd say, 'I think I'd better take you home.' I'd shift into reverse, back out, and drive down the road."

A few months later I happened to see the boy at a social gathering. He walked up to me and said, without introduction, "It happened."

"What happened?" I asked, a total blank. "*It* happened," he said. "How did you know?" He pulled me aside to a more private hallway and said, "It was just like you described it."

"What did you do?" I asked.

"Well, I sat up, reached in my pocket, got the car keys out, started the car, shifted into reverse, and so on! Thanks for making me rehearse it," he said. "I had no idea how strong the feelings would be. If I hadn't thought it through, I'd have made the wrong decision."

Delayed Gratification in Sex and in Economics

It's interesting that our word "economy" comes from the Greek word "oikonomia" which means household and comes from the words for kin and law. Our households are the best places for children to learn about the economies of money (saving, maximizing, valuing, spending wisely) and about the economies of sex.

As mentioned earlier, one goal parents should have is to help teens see sex not as an isolated, "walled-off" topic but as something relevant and connected to everything else, and to help them understand that good principles such as responsibility and delayed gratification apply to sex just as they apply to work or to money or to any other subject. This kind of combining and overlap is part of the point of the following discussion aimed at thirteen- and fourteen-year-olds.

DIALOGUE

Cory, you know that mountain bike you've been wanting?

Cory: Yes.

Well, I've been thinking about it. I think it's something pretty important, and I want to help you get it. I may have a deal for you, but first let's think a little bit about money. How much are you earning (or getting for your allowance) each week?*

Cory: Fifteen dollars.

How much of that could you save, on average, if you really tried?

Cory: Maybe seven-fifty.

Okay. That would be at least thirty dollars saved each month. How much is the bike?

Cory: Three hundred and twenty dollars.

Interesting. Now . . . there are three *secrets* of saving money. Do you want to know what they are?

Cory: Yes.

Okay, the first secret of saving money is to decide on a percentage you want to save whenever you earn any money. Why do you think that would work?

Cory: If you do that, then you can't spend it.

Right. So if you're really going to save fifty percent of your allowance (earnings), what do you need to do?

Cory [clues and help]: Put seven-fifty in savings every time I get fifteen

---

*See *3 Steps to a Strong Family* for ideas on replacing an allowance with a "family economy" that allows kids to earn money.

dollars—right when I get it, before I've spent anything. Put it somewhere and leave it there.

Okay, that is the second secret. You put away that percentage every time you get paid or get your allowance—first thing, before you spend any. Why is that important?

Cory: If you save it first, you can't spend it.

Exactly. Here's the last secret. It's especially for when you're a little older. Don't use credit cards. Do you know what a credit card is?

Cory: [help and clues]: A card you can use to buy things and then pay for them later.

Why would that be bad for saving?

Cory: You'd spend too much. You might spend money before you'd even earned it.

Lots of people do. It's like the opposite of saving. When you get to be eighteen or so, banks will start sending you credit cards or preapproved applications. Take a pair of scissors and cut them in half! When you're older and have more money, a credit card isn't so dangerous. Or you can get a debit card, which allows you to spend only the money you already have in the bank, just like writing a check. If you use those three secrets—pick a percentage to save, always take out your savings first, and don't use credit cards—you'll be rich. I promise. Okay?

Cory: Okay.

And I think I have an idea how you can get that bike, but first, while we're on the subject of saving, let's talk a little more about the most beautiful and awesome thing and how you can save it. First of all, why would you want to save sex?

Cory [help and clues]: Because it's more special with someone you really love, so you should save it until then. Also, sex can be dangerous if you do it too early.

Right. And is it hard or easy to save sex?

Cory: Hard.

Why?

Cory: Because lots of other kids are doing it, and you see it on TV and stuff.

Okay, so there are three secrets for this, too. First, are a boy and girl in any danger of having sex while they're with other people?

Cory: No.

So what would be one sure way not to have sex too early?

Cory: Don't be alone together.

Exactly, Cory. That's the first secret. We think it would be a good idea if you didn't go on dates alone with a girl until you are fifteen or sixteen. We'll talk more about that later, but it's the first secret of saving sex, wouldn't you agree?

Cory: Yes.

Now, what else almost always happens first, before a boy and girl who are too young have sex?

Cory [help and clues]: Taking their clothes off or touching each other in private places.

Exactly. So the second secret is simple. Once you do start dating, keep your clothes on and have some "no-hands zones," places you won't touch and won't allow to be touched. Where are those "no-hands zones"?

Cory [help and clues]: A girl's breasts, bottom, and vagina.

If you're older and dating a girl and you like her, can you kiss her and hug her without touching those parts?

Cory: Yes.

Sure you can. So that's the second secret of saving sex. You keep your hands away from those zones, and you keep your clothes on. The third secret is pretty simple, too. What's one more thing people usually do before they have sex?

Cory [help and clues]: They lay down on a bed or a couch or something.

Right. They get horizontal instead of staying vertical. Do you know those words?

Cory [help and clues]: Vertical is up and down, like sitting up or standing up. Horizontal is side to side, like lying down.

Right. So if you wanted to save sex, what would be a good idea?

Cory: Don't lie down with a girl. Stay sitting up or standing up if you kiss her. Stay vertical, not horizontal.

Exactly, Cory. Those are the three secrets. I promise you that if you don't single-date too early, if you keep your hands off the no-touch zones, and if you stay vertical, not horizontal, when you're with a girl, you'll be able to save sex, and it will get more and more special instead of less and less special. Does that make sense?

Cory: Yes.

Let me tell you a story. In the Old West there was a stagecoach company that wanted to hire a new driver. Three men applied, so they had a contest to see who was the best driver. Each one had to drive the stagecoach up a mountain trail where a big cliff dropped off on one side. Two of the drivers were so skillful that they could get the horses and stagecoach wheels within inches of the edge of the cliff. The third driver didn't try to get close to the edge; he kept both the horses and the wheels clear at the other side of the road, as far as possible from the edge. Who do you think got the job?

Cory: They guy who was safe, who didn't take risks, who stayed as far as possible from the edge.

Yes! How does that apply to the question of sex?

Cory [clues and help]: If you keep the rules—about not dating too soon, no-hands zones, and staying vertical—it's like staying far away from the edge of the cliff.

Exactly! I'm proud of you, Cory. It's fun to talk about this stuff with you. I feel as though I'm talking to my good friend as well as to my son. Let's get back to the money saving part for a minute. How much do you have saved so far?

Cory: Seventy dollars.

Okay, and if you followed those secrets and saved seven dollars and fifty cents every week, which would be at least thirty dollars every month, how many months would it take to save ninety dollars more?

Cory: Three months . . . until June.

Right. So then you'd have one hundred and sixty dollars all together in your bike savings fund. Here's the deal. If you can do it, you'll have half of the money for the bike by June, and I'll pay the other half. Deal?

Cory: Deal!

Bad Reasons and Bad Lines

If your hope and your goal is for your child to wait for sex (whether the term of that waiting is until marriage or until college or whatever), one of the most valuable tools you can give him or her is solid resistance to the poor logic of the reasons kids have sex and to the "lines" kids (particularly boys) use to justify sex. The bad reasons and bad lines can be juxtapositioned against the good reasons and good logic in "waiting."

This discussion ought to take place when your child is fourteen, even if he or she is not dating yet, and earlier if you suspect your child is already exposed to some of the bad reasons and bad lines. It's best if your child hears about and understands the folly and danger of both *before* hearing them from a peer.

DIALOGUE

Renee, we've talked about how sad it is when kids have sex too soon—you know, before they're really in love, before they really know what it means or how special it can be?

Renee: Yes.

Is it the most beautiful, awesome thing in the world when it happens too soon and in the wrong way or the wrong place?

Renee: No.

Besides, it's also . . . what?

Renee: Dangerous!

Right. So why do you think some kids do it?

Renee [help and clues]: They think it's cool, or they want to brag about it, or maybe they're just curious.

Good. Those are some of the reasons. Actually, this book that I have has a list of eleven reasons young kids have given for why they have sex. I'll show them to you, and you see which ones you think are good reasons and which ones you think are bad reasons, okay?

Renee: Okay.

1. Everybody does it.
2. My friends were doing it and making fun of me because I hadn't.
3. From a boy: It's macho. It shows I'm a man!
4. From a girl: Jason said he would dump me if I didn't. I want him to love me.
5. It feels good and it doesn't hurt anybody, so why not?
6. People need sex. It's natural.
7. It looks cool and sounds cool on TV and in the music I like.
8. My parents told me not to.
9. I was bored. And it's more interesting than Nintendo.
10. It's just part of growing up.
11. I love her and she loves me.

Which do you think are good reasons?

Renee: None of them. Well, maybe the last one.

Why not the first ten?

Renee: [help as needed]: They're just dumb. It's as if they think sex is some kind of a game. They don't know it's beautiful and awesome and should be kept for someone special when you're older and when you're really in love.

I agree. What about number eleven? Remember, these are reasons junior high and high school kids give.

Renee: I think they're too young.

How old should they be to use reason eleven?

Renee: Old enough to know you are in love and to get married.

I think so, too. So if these are all bad reasons, what are the good ones? What is a good reason for having sex when you're older?

Renee: To start a baby.

That's a good reason. How old would you have to be to have that reason?

Renee: Old enough to be married and to want to take care of a baby.

Very good. Are there any other good reasons for a married couple to have sex?

Renee: I don't know.

Do you think a married couple should have sex only when they wanted to have a baby?

Renee: No, because it's also to show how much they love each other.

Exactly. When people are old enough to be really, truly in love and want to stay with each other and be loyal and committed to each other, that's when sex can be totally awesome and beautiful. In fact, there's a much better way to say it than "having sex." Do you know a better name for it?

Renee: Making love?

Right! Okay, Renee, now let's talk about one other really important thing. Sometimes when someone wants to have sex or do sexual things for one of the wrong reasons, they say certain things to try to convince the other person to do it. The words a person might say to try to talk another person into having sex are called *lines*. It is usually a boy saying a line to a girl when they're on a date. But it could be the other way around. So what is a line?

Renee: Something said by someone who is trying to make a bad reason sound like a good one.

Exactly! You'll probably hear some of these lines when you're older. So let's role-play some of them now. I'll give you a line, and you tell me what you'd respond to someone who gave you that line. Okay?

Renee: Okay.

Line 1: "If you love me, you'll have sex with me."

Renee: If you love me, you'll respect my feelings and not push me into doing something I'm not ready for.

Line 2: "I know you want to do it. You're just afraid of what people will say."

Renee: If I wanted to do it, I wouldn't be arguing with you about it.

Line 3: "Everybody's doing it."

Renee: That isn't true, and anyway, I'm not everybody. I'm me.

Line 4: "It's just part of growing up."

Renee: Having sex doesn't mean you're grown up. Being grown up to me means deciding what I believe and then sticking to those beliefs.

Line 5: "But I love you . . ."

Renee: Good. Then please respect how I feel.

Line 6: "You want it as much as I do."

Renee: No, I really don't. I have a lot of plans for my life, and I don't want to mess things up by getting pregnant [getting you pregnant].

Line 7: "If you don't, somebody else will."

Renee: If all I mean to you is a body to have sex with, maybe we shouldn't be going out at all. You have no right to use me.

Line 8: "But I have to have it! I need it!"

Renee: No, you don't. What's best for people is doing what they believe is best! I believe it's best to wait.

Line 9: "It doesn't hurt anybody!"

Renee: It could hurt a lot of people, including me!

Line 10: "Give me one good reason why we shouldn't."

Renee: There are lots of good reasons, but I'll just give you one that should be good enough. I don't want to!

Good job, Renee. How did that make you feel?

Renee: Good, as if I was doing what I thought was right and not being pressured into something.

Okay, Renee. Thanks for the talk. Remember, there are lots of reasons for waiting. It's the safest thing. People who really care will respect you more, and it will help you remember that sex is—

Renee: I know, I know, the most beautiful and awesome thing in the world!

If your child is a boy, just change the emphasis. Put a little more attention on "why would you never say any of those lines to anyone?" and a little less on "what would you say if someone tried this line on you?" But cover both sides in either case.

Starting Over

In an ideal world, all parents would have early discussions with their kids about sex, and children would grow up with a healthy attitude, practice sexual restraint and responsibility, and save intimacy for a time when they were mature and committed. In the real world, however, sex frequently happens too early, and kids as well as parents, particularly parents who might read this book, are often left with feelings of guilt and a sense of an irrecoverable loss or an uncorrectable mistake.

Yet there is a trend right now in this country away from this kind of finalism or fatalism. The idea of starting over, sometimes called "secondary virginity" or "revirginating," is catching on with thousands of teens and thousands of families.

The thing to remember is this: If you as a parent have thought the matter through (with or without this book) and have concluded that abstinence until maturity and commitment is best for your child, then that conclusion is equally valid whether or not your child has had previous sexual encounters. And if your child has made or can make a decision that waiting is best, that decision is valuable and useful even if there has been earlier sexual experience. The point is, we can't make decisions about or set goals for the past, only the future.

Don't spend too much time wishing you or your child had behaved differently in the past. Think instead about what is best for the present and the future. Think first about your child's protection if he or she is sexually active, but if you now believe that the best and most complete protection is abstinence, set that as your goal and work toward it. Be realistic and understand that changing an attitude or a behavior pattern is more difficult than building one from scratch, but be assured that it can be done.

If you have already progressed through some of the discussions in this book or had similar talks without the book only to find that your child, previously or recently, has had sexual experience, simply reassure him or her that everything you have talked about is still valid and that while it may be harder, he can start over. Then redouble your efforts to open up the subject and to help your child make reasoned, informed decisions about what is best for his life and for his future.

If your child had sexual experience before you began using this book or had similar discussions, and if you now feel strongly about the benefits of teaching more sexual restraint, you may want to begin with a discussion something like the following.

DIALOGUE

Shirlene, I've been thinking really hard lately about something I want to share with you. All right?

Shirlene: Okay.

Part of it is that I've been reading this book, *How to Talk with Your Child About Sex,* and I've realized how much more I could have told you and discussed with you as you were growing up. If I'd done so, you wouldn't have had to learn as much as you have from friends or media or even from the sexual experience you've had. So first I'd like to apologize for not telling you more, sooner. I love you, Shirlene. Will you accept my apology?

Shirlene: Sure. It's all right.

Shirlene, here's the thing. What I really want to do is kind of start over. Even though you're older and you already know most of what I could tell you about sex, I'd like to go back and talk about some things I wish we'd talked about when you were eight or nine. We could just think of it as a *review,* and I think it would help us feel closer to each other. Would that be okay?

Response. Shirlene may say, "How long will it take?" or "Come on, Mom, I'm not a kid anymore" or "Mom, you know I've already had sex. What would be the point?" Or she may surprise you and simply agree. Whatever the case, reassure her of your genuine interest and love, and impress upon her that you're not making judgments about her past.

The way I look at it, Shirlene, we should both be more interested in the future than in the past. It doesn't do much good for me to feel all guilty about not being a better parent and not talking more with you about sex when you were small. And it wouldn't do much good for you to worry or wonder if you should have done things differently regarding sex. Let's just start over. Will you tell me, first of all, what you think is best for you right now, forgetting the past? Is it best for you to go on having sexual experiences, or do you think it's best to wait until you are older and have a deeper, longer-term relationship with someone?

Response. If Shirlene now wants to wait, continue with this discussion. If not, select some of the essays from chapter 5 to read together or separately, and work toward a mutual conclusion that waiting is the best policy. Reassure her that abstinence or virginity is something that can be regained or reclaimed if that is what a person wants and thinks is best.

Here's an idea. Let's start with a discussion about the facts of life that we could have had when you were eight. I'd like you to imagine that you are eight and say what you think you would have said at age eight. Obviously it won't teach you anything you don't know, but it will review everything and maybe put a new slant or attitude on things, setting the stage for some other, more advanced things about sex that we can talk about. Would that be all right?

Response.

We'll also discuss other things related to sex as a review, and after we've done that, you may want to read some really thoughtful little essays written for kids your age or a little older that might help you make some solid long-term decisions. We'll just take our time and go at your pace, okay?

Shirlene: Okay.

Thanks, Shirlene. I'm excited. I think this will be good for both of us.

If you can get to this point with your child, go through the age eight discussion together and then select together which of the follow-up (chapter 3) and behavioral (chapter 4) discussions are interesting and relevant. Treat them all as a review that will set the stage for starting over with a new, more responsible attitude toward sex and a new appreciation of what sex can still be: "the most beautiful, awesome thing in the world."

Let the review process take a few weeks if necessary. Don't rush it. Progress through them as time and interest allow.

As a parent, read in advance the essays of chapter 5 and decide which ones will appeal most to your child and will have the most influence in terms of increasing his or her desire or strengthening his or her resolve to wait. Explain to your child that these essays were written to help teens make decisions about their own future, regardless of what they may have done in the past. Invite your child to read the ones you have chosen and use the provided discussion questions to talk through the conclusions and your own and your child's opinions.

A Dinner Conversation About Trends in Extramarital and Premarital Sex

"If the social acceptance of premarital sex grows over the next thirty years as it has over the last thirty," said a friend recently, "literally everyone will be having sex with everyone."

We were at a dinner party where I (Richard) often like to take a contrary approach just to make the conversation more interesting. A comparison came to mind that allowed me to take the opposite view.

"I don't think it will go that way," I said. "I think that thirty years from now, one generation from now, sex outside of marriage, especially casual, uncommitted sex, will be much less prevalent in our society than it is today. Monogamy will be the accepted ideal and more and more the societal norm. The bulk of society will resist and resent those who participate in casual or uncommitted sex. It will be something of a social stigma . . ."

Around the table people were staring at me with their mouths open. Was I putting them on? I must be joking. No one was taking me seriously until I finished that sentence: ". . . much like smoking has become today."

Now I had people's attention. I'd started out just to be contrary, but now I was getting excited about the realistic possibilities of my outlandish prediction. "Thirty years ago it was hard and lonely to be a nonsmoker. Pretty much everyone on TV and in the movies smoked. At most parties you felt pretty out of it if you didn't light up. You had to go to tiny nonsmokers' sections on planes or in restaurants. Smoking was more than acceptable, it was fashionable. Everyone did it, so why not you? And a whole big, powerful industry promoted it to us every hour of every day. Oh, we had some evidence that smoking was harmful, statistics and such, but it only hurt *you*. And, hey, it couldn't even hurt you much if you remembered moderation or used filters. Of course many parents still wanted their kids to avoid smoking. They would go out of a child's room to smoke and hope the kids didn't pick up on their habit."

People were ahead of me now. They knew where I was taking the argument. "It's hard to remember those times now that smoking is so passé. Many of us finally admitted what, with hindsight, was obvious: Smoking is a dumb thing to do. It puts you and those closest to you at real and serious risk. Everyone's a victim, and secondhand smoke kills. Our kids are far more likely to smoke if we do. Tobacco giants are finally cast properly—as huge villains."

Some people at the table now looked encouraged, even hopeful; others' eyes were challenging me to complete the analogy successfully. "Think how our attitudes and societal mores on extramarital sex today parallel where we were thirty years ago on smoking. Today it sometimes feels a bit awkward and lonely to believe in and practice fidelity and chastity. Pretty much everyone on TV and in movies jumps into bed. Our parties and our very lifestyles and conversation make casual sex seem like the norm. Everyone does it, so why not you? And a whole birth control complex promotes it. Oh, we have scary statistics on AIDS, teen pregnancy, marriage and family breakup and failure linked to extramarital and casual sex, but if it's between consenting adults, it's a victimless crime. Of course, many parents still want their kids to practice abstinence. We keep our own affairs or addictions out of their view and hope they do what we say and not what we do."

Some people were nodding. Yes, but so what?

"Well, maybe thirty years into the future, adultery and fornication will be as passé as smoking is today. Maybe the majority of us will, with hindsight, finally admit that extramarital, uncommitted sex is dumb. It puts you and those closest to you at risk. For momentary pleasure we risk our emotional and physical health, our trust and confidence, our tenderest commitment, love, and honor, our self-respect. Everyone is a victim. Casual sex kills relationships, kills families, kills unborn children."

I don't know if I convinced anyone that night, perhaps not even myself. But if we feel it is the right thing and the best thing, maybe it isn't something we should wait for. Maybe it is something we should work for.

Most adult parents, given the accumulated wisdom of their experience and the clarity and understanding that come with hindsight, are inclined to say, "I now realize that a committed, loving, long-term monogamous relationship is the best way to live and the best chance to be happy."

More and more, this view is shared even by people generally viewed as advocates of liberal social policy. In an address at Smith College on November 16, 1994, Patricia Ireland, president of the National Organization for Women, concluded that a long-term, committed relationship that is monogamous is a satisfying way to live. She was forty-nine at the time and suggested that her perspective had changed from what she might have thought in her twenties. Then she cautioned that people should not hold out a dream of what they think should be and ignore the consequences of what is.

But the point is, we *can* hold out this dream of what we think should be. That is exactly what we parents need to do: hold out the dreams of what we think is happiest and best for our children, try to raise them in light and truth and hope, try to make our own lives into positive examples for them even if we have to change. The smoking analogy works again as we talk about parental change. If we once smoked but have quit, we want our children not to follow our pattern but to do better—never to start smoking. And if we, in a different time and a different world, engaged in casual sex but no longer do, we want our children not to follow that same pattern but to do better—never to start casual sex.

Few would fault Patricia Ireland—or any head of any big organization with a social agenda—for trying to do what she feels is best for "the consequences of what is." But parents have the privilege, as the personal, loving stewards of young children, to hold out the dream of what they think should be and to work to make that dream a reality.

As only one parent, you're not going to change the sexual norms of society or contain the pornography in media or on the Internet, or bring about legislation to deal with the poverty, alienation, and disease precipitated by uncommitted sex, but you can help your child grow up with a positive attitude about "the most beautiful, awesome thing in the world." You can increase your child's chances of ordering and disciplining his or her life so that sexual involvement follows commitment. And you can improve the odds of your child's having a loving, lasting marriage and a strong, healthy family.

And the interesting thing is, over time and one family at a time, that is exactly how parents can change the world.

5

Discussions of Perspective and Personal Standards with Fifteen- to Nineteen-Year-Olds

The discussions in this chapter are short essays and even poems in a few cases, that are intended to stimulate thought and provide perspective. Each one concludes with follow-up questions designed to promote discussion. You can read one of the essays, then ask your teen to read it, and then discuss it. Or you can read it aloud together. Either way, the tone and the attitude should be that you're exploring together some perspectives about sex and relationships, and this book is a tool that you're using to give you some specific topics to discuss. This kind of open or equal approach shows respect for your teen and shows him that these are issues you deal with, too. It indicates that you value his opinion and think of him as mature enough to discuss these topics together.

Becoming Consultants Rather Than Managers

With older teens, our parental role should shift from that of a manager to that of a consultant. As our sons and daughters progress through and beyond their high school years, we have less and less direct control, but we can actually have more and more opportunity to influence developing outlooks and to guide the thought processes that will determine their lifelong perspectives and behavioral standards.

By reading about and discussing sexual issues in the larger context of social, economic, political, religious, as well as personal perspectives, we can help our teens have the context and framework within which to make good personal decisions and to see more clearly how their sexual behavior now will affect their personal lives and families later on.

The objectives of this final chapter are twofold: First, to help our older teens sort out the options, responsibilities, and consequences of their sexual behavior with the kind of perspective and clarity that will maximize their chances of making good choices. Second, to help us parents clarify our own views on what level of restraint is best for our children even as we reassess our own attitudes and behavior.

Exactly how you use this final chapter will depend a lot on the interest level and the nature and academic capacity of your child. If you have a high school student who reads well and tests well, you may want to point out that some of the readings and essays are not unlike the reading sections of the S.A.T., A.C.T., or other college entrance tests. Ask your child to read for comprehension and view the discussion questions as a kind of quiz as well as an opportunity to form an opinion on the perspectives and views presented.

On the other hand, if the academic angle is the surest way *not* to interest your child, you might approach the readings simply as interesting articles about sex. The topic alone is usually enough to generate initial interest.

However you approach it, there are a few important guidelines:

1. Read each passage thoroughly yourself first and formulate your own opinions. Then either read it aloud together or invite your son or daughter to read it. Be sure you and your child have digested it before you go to the discussion questions. Go over difficult words or terms together.

2. Don't dominate the follow-up talk with your own opinions. Ask the discussion questions and give your child time to respond.

3. Don't feel that you have to come to any particular conclusion or consensus on any of the readings or that you have to finish discussing each one in a single sitting. Go as far as you have time for and then return to it later. The articles are intended not for one open-and-shut talk but for extending the ongoing open communication about sex (and other subjects that it leads to) within your family.

The sequence of these readings is fairly general, and their length and difficulty are varied. Some (particularly the poems at the end) are only a page long, while others run to several pages. Use them at your discretion, according to need and interest and how much time you have.

Remember that "too soon" is better than "too late." Early assimilation of this material by your child will be helpful in his decisions concerning sexual restraint and responsibility.

Reading #1: Evolving Changes in How We Think About Sex—a Pendulum with Two Extremes

Humans in all locations and in all societies have always had sexual mores and rules with formal mating or marriage ceremonies and commitments. Indiscriminate mating or sexual activity has always been condemned. This is attributable at least partly to the human capacity for cause-and-effect reasoning which determined that children need and deserve parents and a nurturing family structure to grow up in, and that any kind of community and economy requires some basic building block of organization—namely the family unit.

In the last hundred years, the pendulum of sexual permissiveness has swung rather widely. The word "Victorian" brings to mind impressions of highly repressive sexual practices: closed-mindedness, attitudes of prudery and intolerance, and sex never being discussed publicly. Sex was a secret subject, meant to be completely reserved, along with all of its preliminaries, for the marriage bed. Women's virtue was so highly prized that it was debatable whether it was preferable for them to lose their lives rather than their virtue. Of course, all sorts of social perversions went on behind the proper, respectable appearances, and men's "indiscretions" were often winked at, considered unavoidable needs or necessities. Still, the tone, the atmosphere, and the one-word description of accepted sexual reality was *repression*.

An essentially Victorian attitude persisted in this country into the 1950s. What we call today "being sexually active" was then called "sin" or, if pregnancy occurred, "being in trouble." The double standard continued, with men getting away with more (of everything except blame) than women. Respectable girls were expected to "hold off" boys, to make them wait and make them commit to marriage, to fidelity, to children, to support, to family. If this waiting didn't happen, it was often considered the woman's fault. A man's sexual "needs" were acknowledged (and his resulting "improprieties" forgiven). A woman's were not. Repression created a lot of dishonesty, a lot of guilt. Clearly there was a need for a sexual revolution.

In the 1960s we got one. But it was the wrong revolution!

What we needed was a sexual revolution that made men and women equal not in their promiscuity but in their commitment to see sex as part of real love, as a beautiful and natural passion of both sexes, and as something that should be an integral part of strengthening and deepening the relationship of two people totally committed to each other.

The worst way to achieve equality is to bring everyone down to a lower level. The best way is to bring everyone up to a higher level. We got the worst. The Victorian double standard that said "men can cheat but women can't" needed a revolution. The new norm we needed was not "men can cheat, so woman can, too," it was "men shouldn't cheat for exactly the same reasons that women shouldn't cheat."

So what we got in the sixties was the wrong sexual revolution. It replaced closed repression with open promiscuity. And for all its rhetoric about liberating women and making them equal with men, it actually victimized women further. It reduced women from trying to ensure and protect virtue, marriage, family, and commitment (by saying "no") to simply trying to protect themselves from AIDS or STDs (by saying "yes, but please use a condom").

The Victorian pendulum needed to swing, but as is often the case with pendulums, it swung too far. It swung from sex that was repressive, judgmental, unequal, and often exploitive to sex that is recreational, casual, and irresponsible (and still unequal and exploitive). The real problem is that both extremes of the pendulum's swings are essentially and profoundly *naive*. In Victorian thinking, people had their heads in the sand, trying to see and hear no evil. Today we have our heads in other sand, ignoring the personal consequences and the far-reaching ramifications of irresponsible sex both before and after marriage.

DISCUSSION

Question: Why have human societies always had sexual rules and marriage ceremonies and commitments?

Answer: Children need nurturing parents to survive, and communities and economies need the basic building block of families.

Question: Which does the author prefer: Victorian attitudes toward sex or today's attitudes toward sex?

Answer: Neither. They are posed as two extremes in the swing of a pendulum.

Question: What does the article imply was wrong with the sexuality and sexual attitudes of Victorian times?
Answer: Hypocrisy and a double standard.

Question: What are the worst and best ways to achieve equality?
Answer: The worst way: Bring everyone down to a lower level. The best way: Bring everyone up to a higher level.

Question: In which of these two ways did the sexual revolution of the 1960s move toward equality?
Answer: It brought people down to the level of "men can cheat, so women can, too." It replaced closed repression with open promiscuity.

Question: If the 1960s was the "wrong revolution," what would have been the right one?
Answer: One that made men and women equal, not in their promiscuity but in their commitment to make sex a part of deep and lasting love.

Question: Which is the most naive, Victorian thinking or today's thinking?
Answer: Both. Victorians ignored hypocrisy. We ignore consequence.

Question: Do you think the article accurately portrays the results of the sexual revolution?

Question: What is your opinion of the article?

Question: What relevance does it have to you?

Reading #2: The Three Broad Levels of Sexual Function, Fulfillment, and Freedom

It is common and accepted, on issues of sex, to say how complex it all is, how there are no simple answers, and how there are no answers that apply to all people or all situations. We often hear that "no two couples are alike, no two sets of circumstances are alike. What's right for one is wrong for another. There are no absolutes. And on and on." It seems that people approach sex in a million different ways and have sex for a million different reasons.

Well, maybe not! It's a complex issue in the sense that it has many dimensions and ramifications, but it's also a personal issue, and when it is thought of that way—as a basic individual choice that each person makes—it can be simplified, brought to its essence, and dealt with intelligently and positively. We can get to the heart of the personal issues of sex by asking a three-pronged question: What is the best kind of sex, what is the worst, and what is in between?

Consensus is actually pretty easy on these questions. Regardless of their politics, their religion, or even their personal marital situations, most mature adults agree that monogamous, long-term, supportive relationships between people who love and are committed to each other are the best settings for the most fulfilling (as well as the most thrilling) kind of sex. It's even easier to agree on the worst kind of sex. Apart from the abnormal atrocities of rape, incest, prostitution, or other crimes, the worst "normal" sex is cheating, extramarital, family-and-marriage-breaking affairs involving married adults; and indiscriminate, promiscuous, experimental, or exploitive "too-early" sex involving children and teens. Admittedly, these are broad categories with a lot of subgroups, but most people share a similar vision of happily married, committed, spouse-nourishing sex as "best," and of immature or casual high-risk sex as "worst." In between, of course, is a range of semi-committed, semi-safe sex.

We're not dealing here with the complexities of what is possible or what is likely or even with what is currently going on. We're dealing simply with what is best and what is worst and what is in between. If we could name these three categories—the best (to be admired and pursued), the worst (to be avoided and combated), and the middle (to be seen for what it is and hopefully improved on)—we could build a model and a terminology that would help in approaching and dealing with the entire subject and the complete issue.

The "best" category needs a name that implies nourishment, fulfillment, security, supportive loyalty, and the deepest kind of love. The "worst" needs a name meaning immature, base, undisciplined, even animalistic. And the "middle" needs a name that suggests partly bad and partly good, but something that is inconsistent and unpredictable.

Perhaps a useful name for the best kind of marital intimacy is "wholesex." And maybe we could call the worst kind "lowsex." What is in between might be called "halfsex." Think for a minute about the implications and double meanings of each word.

"Whole" implies health as well as completeness—an integrated, connected, win-win kind of relationship in which physical sex is part of the larger whole of emotional and spiritual love and oneness.

"Half" implies partly full and partly empty, incompleteness, not-full-ness. What is felt is half love and half lust. There is love and loyalty and commitment, but each is conditional and therefore partial. In these relationships there are always half-truths, half-trust, halfhearted promises. Half implies a surface-only quality, a diluted nature, a subtle selfishness, and a separateness and distance from full, unrestricted, other-centered love. And the real problem with "half" is that in its separateness it often functions like less than half, as in half a pair of scissors.

"Low" suggests various combinations of low maturity, low respect (for self and others), low discipline, low potential, and low chances of success, fulfillment, or permanence. It is also low as in the "low-road," as in subtly devious and dishonest. And it is low in terms of an instinctive animalistic approach rather than a reasoned human approach.

Wholesex exists as a current reality for some and as a feasible, potential reality for everyone. It is only beyond reach for those who don't want it or choose not to pursue it. Wholesex isn't perfect. It's not consistently compatible or pleasantly predictable (indeed, those qualities might undermine its essential element of excitement and variety). But it is something that two people in love are willing to commit to and live for. It becomes wholesex the minute those commitments are complete. It will have its ups and downs, its pleasures and its pains, but it will stay wholesex because of its true vows. And it will, over time, enhance happiness, provide peace, extend a circle of family security, and even extend life.

Lowsex is epidemic in our society. It is promoted in so many ways by so much of the media—sometimes for motives as simple as profit and sometimes for motives as complex as self-justification and even "misery loves company." Lowsex exists in countless alternatives and infinite variety, while wholesex always has basic, common elements. Lowsex is as varied as whole sex is singular. All wholesex relationships are the same in that they have commitment. All lowsex encounters are unique in how they hurt, how they scar, and how they pull down.

Halfsex, as the name implies, is often neither the product of positive planning and design nor of negative, exploitive manipulation. Usually it just happens. There is enough love to link but not enough to bond. There is enough commitment for short- or mid-term loyalty but not for long- or life-term loyalty. People grasp and are grateful for the love they find but are either unable, unaware, unwilling, or unsure when it comes to extending that love and making it exclusive. It gets them through thin but not through thick, mirroring the ultimately shallow depth of their feelings.

Like most worthwhile things in life, wholesex requires risk. It is the incredible emotional risk of giving yourself totally, without reservation or time limit, to another person. It involves intentionally not leaving yourself a back door or a test period or even a prenuptial agreement. It disallows the possibility of long-term failure because it is unwilling to entertain any conditions for giving up.

Some practitioners of lowsex seek to justify or rationalize it by claiming that it provides freedom, which is defined as "not being tied down" or (most accurately and most ironically) as "being uncommitted." Yet lowsex is actually an intense and dangerous form of bondage. It is the bondage of alienation, of regret, of guilt, of consequences. It is the antithesis of the true freedom that comes with wholesex (freedom from sickness, from loneliness, and from the worry of who might be hurt, and how).

Those who find themselves in halfsex relationships sometimes argue (perhaps trying to convince themselves) that there is fulfillment in moving through a series of partial or short-term commitments (serial monogamy) in pursuit of a better and more lasting one. Their argument actually concedes that more fulfilling wholesex is the destination to which they hope their journey through halfsex will lead. Yet, without a paradigm change, it rarely does.

We live in a world where so many of us have become sophisticated at goal setting and planning, at determining what we want economically and materially, and going after it in a dedicated and disciplined way. We have learned to be proactive and take the offensive in terms of what we want to own and who we want to be. Yet we are often remarkably reactionary, defensive, and even pawnlike when it comes to the relationships in our lives. We drift into them, we follow "norms" without questioning them, and suddenly we find ourselves in places we never planned to be. The surest path to a wholesex relationship is simply to set it as a goal, to settle for nothing less, to avoid lowsex like the plague that it is, and to refuse halfsex opportunities whenever they confront us.

DISCUSSION

Question: True or false: The writer of this essay thinks the subject of sex is a hopelessly complex issue for which there are no simple or universal answers.

Answer: False. The author believes it can be simplified in a very useful and important way.

Question: What is the "three-pronged" question that can simplify the personal issues of sex?
Answer: What is the best kind of sex, what is the worst, and what is in between?

Question: Other than sex crimes, what are the two most damaging and "worst" kinds of sex?
Answer: Cheating or extramarital affairs and experimental or casual sex involving children or teens.

Question: What is the most fulfilling, "best" kind of sex?
Answer: A monogamous, committed, long-term relationship.

Question: What does monogamy mean?
Answer: Two people in a committed and loyal relationship with each other. Marriage is the best example.

Question: What names does the author give to the best, worst, and in-between types of sexual relationships and practices? What meanings and implications do these names have?
Answer: Wholesex, lowsex, and halfsex. The meanings and implications are on pages 174 to 176.

Question: Which of the three brings the most freedom? The least risk? The most rewards? Why?
Answer: Wholesex.

Question: What arguments do people make to justify lowsex or halfsex? Are they good arguments?
Answer: Freedom, experience; see page 176.

Question: How does one pursue the goal of wholesex?
Answer: See the concluding paragraph of the article.

Question: What do you think of the essay? Do you agree with its main points? Does it oversimplify? Is it relevant to you now?

Reading #3: Recreation or Consummation

Sex can be viewed, particularly by an unmarried single individual, from varying perspectives. Placing these perspectives on a spectrum, sex is thought of, at one extreme, as an activity. It is perceived as a need to be filled, a challenge to be met, a pleasure to sample, a form of exercise in which to increase capacity or fitness, or a relaxation in which to indulge. In each of these cases it is a form of recreation, something you do for yourself and as an end in itself. It is not particularly important who you do it with, although, as with most recreation, an attractive and competent partner probably makes it more enjoyable. Like most games there is often a winner and a loser, but either way, there's probably another chance tomorrow.

At the other extreme, sex is considered the highest level of intimacy and a powerful symbol of a committed joining, a consummation, an act that seals, solemnizes, commits, and makes something lasting, complete, and final. It brings to fruition a courtship and celebrates and symbolizes the oneness of marriage. At this extreme it is something you do for someone you love more than for yourself, and it is a means to ever deeper love and a "strengthener" of emotional and spiritual feelings. It is totally important who it is with because it is only and exclusively with that person.

In between recreation and consummation on the spectrum are all kinds of combinations and compromises. As we move across the spectrum from recreation to consummation, we move away from temporary, instant gratification and toward more lasting, delayed gratification. We move away from danger and toward safety, away from sickness and toward health, away from deceit and toward trust, away from selfishness and toward selflessness, away from lust and toward love, away from taking and toward giving, away from roughness and toward tenderness, away from win-lose competition and toward win-win synergy, away from the insecure need to prove ourselves and toward the secure acceptance of ourselves, away from separateness and toward oneness, away from repetition and desensitization and toward romance and excitement, away from fragile families and toward secure, strong ones.

Another way to view the spectrum—perhaps the most important way—is in terms of family and its effect on family.

Studies show that well over 95 percent of adult Americans name family as their highest priority. When sex is thought of as a subset of family or as an influence on family, we begin to see it in its truest and most revealing light.

The concept is simple. Think of the same spectrum but with the added, overlaid element of the strength and endurance of families. The farther we move toward loyal, committed, monogamous sex, the more we build, strengthen, protect, and preserve families. The farther we move toward recreational, experimental, or casual sex, the more we prevent, endanger, disrupt, and destroy families.

DISCUSSION

Question: What does the word "consummation" mean?
Answer: Complete, fulfilled, the highest or the best.

Question: Do the sentiments of this essay agree or disagree with those of the preceding essay? How do the terms or names used by the authors compare?
Answer: Agree. Wholesex equals consummation; lowsex equals recreation.

Question: What are the basic differences between sex as recreation and sex as consummation?

Answer: One is temporary and an end in itself. The other is lasting and the means to deeper love.

Question: Draw your own spectrum—a long line with "recreation" at one end and "consummation" at the other. Write the following words at one end of the spectrum or along the line according to where they "fit": danger, health, trust, selfishness, lust, giving, safety, love, sickness, deceit, selflessness, taking, tenderness, separateness, roughness, oneness, repetition, romance, stronger family, weaker family.

Question: How is this article relevant to you now and in the future?

Reading #4: Statistics and the Broader Perspective

Within this essay, relevant statistics are arranged in four groups of realities and trends:

1. Sexual Activity: the rapid increases in casual sex, teen pregnancy, and sexually transmitted diseases at ever younger ages.
2. Sexual Victims: the harm and damage being done, particularly to women, children, and families.
3. Sexual Attitudes: the dramatic change in our views of some aspects of sex but not others, and one massive attitude change that affects nearly everyone.
4. Sexual Messages: media's disproportionate and deceptive influence and the profound difference between immorality and amorality.

Each group of statistics is followed by a brief commentary and by discussion questions. This reading may be broken down into as many as four separate discussions.

SEXUAL ACTIVITY

Realities

- "Sexually transmitted diseases and unwanted pregnancies are found in alarmingly high numbers in progressively younger adolescents."[1]
- In 1996, 73 percent of young men and 56 percent of young women had experienced sexual intercourse by their eighteenth birthday (at age seventeen or younger), up from 55 percent and 35 percent in 1970.[2]
- Sexual intercourse among fifteen-year-old girls went from 4.6 percent in 1970 to 25.6 percent in 1988 and continues to climb today.[3]
- Today, 21 percent of female twelfth graders and 25 percent of male twelfth graders have had four or more sex partners.[4]
- Each year more than one million U.S. teenagers become pregnant (and 400,000 have abortions). Three million acquire sexually transmitted diseases (that is one out of six who are sexually active).[5]
- U.S. teen pregnancy rates continually surpass those of all other developed countries. Our rate of teen pregnancy is ten times that of Japan or the Netherlands.[6]
- Every year the teen pregnancy rate in San Francisco is significantly lower than any other major metropolitan area in the United States due to the strong family orientation of its large Asian-American population.[7]

Commentary

National leaders have called teen pregnancy the nation's "most serious social problem"[8] with good reason. The economic ramifications are highlighted by the fact that 50 percent of teens who give birth are on welfare within one year.[9] The emotional and social costs can't be measured by any statistics, and involvement in early sex is closely linked to the school dropout rate and drug use.[10] Sexual activity happens earlier and earlier to more and more kids, and one-sixth of those it "happens to" acquire a sexually transmitted disease.

How things have turned upside down in the last forty years can be illustrated by comparing pollsters' concerns in the 1950s (when they could not get accurate "virginity percentages" because those polled did not want to admit they had had sex) to pollsters' concerns today (those polled do not want to admit they haven't had sex). A recent teenage guest on ABC's *Nightline* said, "I am a freshman at a high school in California, and the pressure I feel to have sex is incredible. I am not yet ready to have sex, but I feel that I need to do so so that this intense amount of pressure is lifted."[11]

While 75 percent of males under eighteen have had sexual intercourse, only 25 percent have had four or more sexual partners. Among girls the percentages are 56 percent and 21 percent. Clearly, substantial numbers (half of boys and a third of girls) are "trying" sex but not pursuing it to promiscuous levels or going from partner to partner. Many, like the teen on *Nightline,* are just "doing it" to remove the perceived social stigma of virginity.

The sheer numbers and percentages of teens involved in sex and subject to physical disease and emotional damage are shocking and worrisome. The progressively younger age at which children are getting involved may be even worse news.

The beliefs and traditions of families and the mores of the broader society are the prime determinants of young people's sexual activity.

DISCUSSION

Question: What is the most frightening thing shown by the first group of statistics?

Answer: That kids are sexually active at ever younger ages.

Question: Why is teen pregnancy and teen sexual activity such a significant economic problem?

Answer: Fifty percent of teen mothers are on welfare, 400,000 teens get abortions each year, and three million get sexually transmitted diseases. All these are costly economically as well as socially and personally.

Question: In light of these statistics, is the phrase "everyone's doing it" accurate?

Answer: No. Seventy percent of fifteen-year-old girls and 46 percent of eighteen-year-olds are virgins.

Question: Why do you think the U.S. teen pregnancy rate is the highest in the world?

Question: Why is the San Francisco teen pregnancy rate the lowest of major U.S. cities?

Question: If family teachings are the key to avoiding early sex and teen pregnancy (as the San Francisco statistic suggests), how good are your chances of avoiding both?

Answer: Pretty good—since I'm in this family.

Question: What do you think of the statement by the girl on *Nightline*? Have you felt that kind of pressure? What do you do to withstand or combat that pressure?

Question: What do you personally think are some of the most alarming things about these statistics on sexual activity?

SEXUAL VICTIMS: WOMEN, CHILDREN, MARRIAGES, AND FAMILIES

Realities

- When more than one thousand teenage girls in Atlanta were asked what they most wanted to learn in sex education, 84 percent answered, "How to say no without hurting the other person's feelings."[12] These girls, sixteen and younger, were choosing from a list of twenty sex-related topics.

- Two-thirds of high-school-age mothers had a sexual partner who was more than four years older.[13] More than half of the fathers of kids born to eleven- to fifteen-year-olds were over eighteen. Only one-fourth of men who impregnate women under eighteen are under eighteen themselves.[14]

- Married couples who cohabitated before marriage are 33 percent more likely to divorce than couples who did not live together prior to marriage. Virgin brides are significantly less likely to divorce than women who were sexually active before marriage. Virgin grooms are equally unlikely to divorce. Couples who live together without being engaged or married are more likely to use cocaine and other drugs than they were before they moved in together, and live-in boyfriends are more likely to beat their partners than are spouses. Accordingly, Harvard sociologist Christopher Jencks says that premarital sex "may ultimately prove to be a little like smoking dope in the 1960s. In retrospect, maybe it isn't so good for you after all."[15]

- The more sexual activity individuals engage in before marriage, the more likely they are to divorce.[16]

- Multiple surveys indicate that premarital abstinence, not sexual experience, is associated with greater marital sexual satisfaction.[17]

- In the 1950s, nine in ten young women got married without having lived with their partner, compared with one in three in the early 1990s.[18]

Commentary

Young girls are frequently victims of older male predators or of pressure put on them by older partners. Girls who don't really want to have sex often do so to buy acceptance, approval, and affection, and to escape peer pressure by conforming. More than eight out of ten would like to be able to say no. Women are victimized because the formerly common female position of saying, "Please, let's wait for commitment (or marriage or true love or family)" has been changed to saying, "Please wear a condom." Traditionally, men tried to speed things up sexually, while women held them back. Earlier sex is the masculinization of a relationship; it makes commitment take a backseat to gratification.

The stability of families is jeopardized in obvious ways by sexual activity outside of marriage, which destroys trust, undermines loyalty, and breeds fear and insecurity. As one woman said, "The safe sex jingle, 'You're sleeping with everyone your lover has ever slept with,' has added resonance now. You're sharing emotional space with those ex-girlfriends. The acceptance of premarital sex makes it very difficult to sustain the fantasy that we are loved alone."[19]

The widely accepted notion that it is smart and prudent to "try each other out" before committing to marriage turns out to be wrong. Prior cohabitation endangers marriages rather than strengthening them. And of all trends and statistical shifts in the area of sex, the most extreme and dramatic is the percentage of couples living together before marriage. One in ten in the 1950s has become two in three today, an increase of over 600 percent.

Premarital sex, especially casual and recreational sex in the teen years, is the single strongest predictor and precursor of extramarital sex and marital infidelity, which in turn is the most common cause of divorce. And divorce is the factor most directly related to substance abuse, school dropout, teen pregnancy, teen suicide, abuse, adolescent crime and violence, and a host of other social problems. In this light, everyone is a victim.

Marriages and long-term relationships are often the first victims because premarital sex may act to circumvent the process of getting to know someone. When a couple jumps into bed, their relationship takes a monumental leap in intimacy. The couple may bypass important steps in the development of their relationship, such as the discovery of shared interests, trust, and emotional intimacy.

DISCUSSION

Question: Do you think most teenage girls who have sex really want to, or are they being pressured into it (boy pressure and peer pressure)? Which statistic backs up your view?

Answer: Eighty-four percent want to know how to say no without hurting the boy's feelings.

Question: Do statistics bear out the common belief that it's wise to "try out" a partner before marriage?

Answer: No. Divorce is 33 percent more likely among couples who cohabitated before marriage than among those who did not. And drug use and abuse are also more common in couples who lived together before marriage.

Question: What is the largest statistical shift in sexual practices since the 1950s?

Answer: Couples living together prior to marriage—a 600 percent increase.

Question: How does the Harvard sociologist compare premarital sex today with smoking dope in the 1960s?

Answer: Neither is good for you after all.

Question: Who do you think are the real "sexual victims"?

Question: How do the statistics in this group affect your thinking about sex?

SEXUAL ATTITUDES

Realities

- Seventy-four percent of parents have "serious qualms" about their children having sex before marriage.[20]
- Eighty percent of married Americans report that they have never had an extramarital affair.[21]
- For the past twenty-five to thirty years there has been almost no change in how Americans view adultery and teenage sex. A substantial majority think both are always, or almost always, wrong.[22]
- While fewer people are expressing tolerance toward extramarital sex, attitudes about "adult" premarital sex are getting more permissive.[23]

Commentary

More than 80 percent of married parents have never had an extramarital affair, and irrespective of our own sexual activity before marriage and how "liberal" we might consider ourselves to be, three out of four parents wish and hope that their children could avoid premarital sex. An old joke among sex educators is that a conservative is a liberal with a teenage daughter.

Americans' attitudes concerning what is sexually wrong are very similar to the attitudes of twenty-five or thirty years ago, with one glaring exception. According to *U.S. News and World Report*[24]:

> One definite casualty of the sexual revolution: Americans' long-held conviction that virginity should be relinquished only in the marriage bed. To be sure, America has never been sexually pristine. Since the first settlers arrived, lots of unwed teens and young adults took a roll or two in the hay. And there was always a perceived double standard for men, who were expected to "sow their oats,"

and women, who were expected to save themselves for their husbands. Yet there are fundamental differences between the premarital sex of the 1960s and earlier eras and that of the 1990s. In the mid-1960s, many more women were virgins at marriage than is now the case, and men and women who did engage in premarital sex often did so with their betrothed. Cohabitation was comparatively rare, and "shotgun weddings" for pregnant brides were common.

Not only have we given up the ideal of virginity, we've collectively decided that giving it up provides real benefits. The article continues:

> The *U.S. News* poll shows that the majority of respondents under the age of 45 think that adult premarital sex generally benefits people quite apart from the issue of expanding their sexual pleasure. Unlike their elders, younger adults widely endorsed the sowing-one's-oats rationale for premarital sex, so long as the sowing is not done promiscuously. Less than half of those under 45 thought it was a good idea for adults to remain virgins until they marry. And a majority of respondents agreed that having had a few sexual partners makes it easier for a person to pick a compatible spouse.

This type of thinking ignores the emotional trauma and self-esteem risk—not to mention the physical risks—of premarital sex. And the facts are opposite from the expectations. Women who are not virgins at marriage have a significantly higher chance of divorce than virgins.

There is a huge inconsistency and a dangerous irony in tolerating and even claiming benefits for premarital sex while decrying and condemning extramarital sex. It is simply this: Premarital sex is the most consistent predictor of extramarital sex. Those involved in one are more likely to be involved in the other.

DISCUSSION

Question: Do most married people have affairs?

Answer: No. More than 80 percent of married adults have not had an affair.

Question: Do most parents just expect their children to have sex before marriage?

Answer: Seventy-four percent of parents have serious qualms about premarital sex for their kids and wish they would avoid it.

Question: What is the glaring difference in America's attitude toward sex now and thirty years ago?

Answer: Americans still think extramarital sex and teen sex is wrong, but adult premarital sex is now perceived as okay or even beneficial.

Question: What's wrong with this attitude?

Answer: Adult premarital sex is physically and emotionally dangerous and often leads to extramarital sex.

Question: How do these statistics affect your own personal attitudes toward sex?

SEXUAL MESSAGES

Realities

- According to an extensive 1996 poll, just 38 percent of the Hollywood elite (producers, directors, and so on) were concerned about how TV depicted premarital sex, compared with 83 percent of the general public.[24]
- Prime-time network TV shows air as many as eight depictions of premarital sex for every one of sex between married couples. And when premarital sex is depicted, concern about consequences is raised in only 5 percent of cases. "What was once considered as deviant behavior is now treated as the norm."[25]

- Sexual content aired during prime time on television has quadrupled during the past twenty years.[26]

Commentary

Contemporary media (movies, TV, and music) are a classic case of a powerful and disproportionately influential *minority* masquerading as a *majority*. More than we care to admit, our own practices and attitudes are shaped by what we perceive to be the norm. The media portrays premarital sex, casual sex, and semi-committed sex as the norm (and as being without consequences). People find themselves adopting certain sexual attitudes and practices not because they have logically and reasonably decided that it is best (or even that it is what they want) but because "everyone is doing it."

Without parents pulling in a different direction, children accept the "advice" that the media and the peer group give them. And all too often that advice is "If it feels good, do it," "Live for now, pursue instant gratification," "Don't talk about or even worry about consequences," "Sex is recreation," and "Something's wrong with you if you don't do it."

DISCUSSION

Question: What does "a minority masquerading as a majority" mean?

Answer: The directors and producers of Hollywood are much less concerned about the media's portrayal of casual and premarital sex than is the general public. The small number of people who produce the media makes us think that most people are "like them" and not "like us."

Question: Do you think the media influence public and individual behavior or just reflect it?

Question: What do the media usually leave out in their portrayals of premarital or extramarital sex?

Answer: Consequences.

Question: How influenced do you want to be by the media?

Question: What can you do to prevent the media norms from influencing how you live your life?

Reading #5: Culprits

The statistics of the previous essay beg a question: Why, if their consequences are so dire, are extramarital and premarital sex so rampant? People don't set out to destroy their families or to shackle themselves with unwanted pregnancy and the no-win dilemma of abortion. It's not a logical choice to expose ourselves to physical disease and emotional stress and distress. Sexual urges and temptations are strong, but they have always been, and we're probably more aware of the consequences of promiscuous sex than ever before. So why are the numbers and the costs going up? And why is the average age of those getting involved going down? Why do we collectively pay lip service to marital fidelity and sexual responsibility, and yet have more and more people involved in casual or recreational sex?

What is the cause? Who are the culprits? There are at least five:

1. The pornography industry. Those who produce and distribute pornography must shoulder blame. "Porn" means evil or prostitution, and "graphy" means writing or visuals. Pornography promotes casual and recreational sex, even exploitive and predatory sex, and it undermines the value of waiting for true commitment.

2. The broader media. The favored claim of movies, music, television, and other media—that they do not influence society, they only reflect it—is a crock, a transparent, self-serving rationalization. The insidious element here is that much of today's media is essentially a minority masquerading as a majority. And the device is more *amorality* than *immorality*. By

implying that everyone cheats and everyone goes to bed on the first date, and by failing to show real consequences, the media makes casual sex look like the norm and makes those who practice and pursue chastity and fidelity feel out of step and old-fashioned. The advertising media, endlessly using sex to sell, is part of this culprit.

3. The birth control complex. While often well intentioned and always under the noble-sounding guise of "protection," those who sell birth control to children either in the marketing sense or in the advisory sense are facilitating and fueling recreational sex among younger and younger segments of society.

4. Comprehensive sex education programs. Sex education that goes too far—that goes beyond maturation and mechanics, that tries essentially to train kids in sex without sufficient emphasis on responsibility, discipline, or the ideal of a committed marriage—often provokes participation in early, experimental sex that opens up many avenues of serious problems.

5. The general mentality of rationalization and justification. The more "normal" and "average" and "widespread" casual sex becomes or is perceived, the more justified people feel about their own involvement. It is as though we were saying, "Ten million adulterers can't be wrong" or "The fifty percent of high school girls who are sexually active couldn't be completely off track." The "majority" who either practice or condone casual, uncommitted, or semi-committed sex have a certain persuasive power over everyone else. Anything that is accepted and has momentum tends to move and to grow.

These are five culprits, and there may be more. If we want to fight against them, where do we attack? Which culprits do we go after? Should we sue pornographers, boycott objectional media, and oppose comprehensive sex ed and the availability and implied sanction of condoms? Yes, we probably should, as time and opportunity permit. But we can do something far more important and far more effective over time in society. We can commit our own lives to the beauty of committed, consummate sex within marriage, and we can teach this view to our children. If enough of us do this, the general mentality will slowly change and the majority will slowly shift.

DISCUSSION

Question: What conclusion does the author draw?

Answer: People can make their own individual commitments to do what is right, and when enough do, we will change the world.

Question: How does the author of this essay tie it to the statistics of the previous essay?

Answer: By asking the question: "If the statistical consequences of out-of-marriage sex are so bad, why is it increasing?"

Question: Do you agree that the five "culprits" listed each deserve some of the blame for increasing extramarital and premarital sex?

Question: Which culprit(s) do you think is the worst?

Question: Which of the culprits affect you personally? What can you do to avoid them or combat them?

Reading #6: Changing the *F* to a *V*— What Is Really Safe?

Outside of marriage, "safe sex" is at best an oxymoron and at worst a deceptive, devious, dangerous lie. Condoms don't always work either in preventing pregnancy or in preventing disease, and even when they do, casual sex is anything but safe emotionally.

What is truly safe—and what goes beyond safe to exciting and gratifying over the long term—is to *save* sex. Changing that *f* to a *v* makes all the difference. Even if safe sex were realistic, do we really want a goal for which the highest hope is to avoid disease, to avoid unwanted pregnancy, to keep bad or dangerous things from happening to us? Isn't there a higher realm of thinking where our goals have to do with positive things we want to happen rather than with negative things we want not to happen? Trying to avoid harm is like going into a basketball game or a tennis match with the goal of not spraining an ankle or not having a heart attack. How about the goal of winning? How about the goal of joy? How about, in the area of intimacy and sex, the goal of a secure and beautiful relationship of commitment that lasts for a long time, even a lifetime?

Once we raise our goal and our consciousness to this level, safe sex seems not only unrealistic and risky, it seems shallow, foolish, and extremely shortsighted. The goal, particularly for this generation, should not be *safe* sex but to *save* sex.

Replacing the *f* with a *v* can be symbolic. "F" stands for fallacy and frustration and failure as well as for fornication and another *f* word that symbolizes the coarseness and crassness associated with casual, uncommitted sex. *V* stands for value and values, for virtue and even for virginity, that old-fashioned word which actually has more relevance and wisdom in today's world than it ever has before. *V* also stands for victory over self and the kind of discipline and delayed gratification that is always part of saving and that is indispensable to the deepest kinds of happiness.

Saving is essentially the opposite of spending. In the economic sense, those who save carefully are always better off in the long run than those who spend indiscriminately. Spending produces brief, small pleasures. Saving provides the power and joy of something big and lasting.

In the area of sexual intimacy, we think far too little about the long term. The short-term benefits of saving sex are physical and emotional safety, higher self-esteem, and a better chance of early success and achievement in everything from academics to career. But the long-term benefits are even greater. By saving sex we increase our chances (quantitatively and statistically) for a lasting marriage. We lay the foundation of loyalty, commitment, and discipline that will assist us in building a strong family of our own and having a spouse and children who will be the core of our happiness throughout our lives.

Wearing a condom to ensure safe sex is like buying bankruptcy insurance in order to make irresponsible, indiscriminate spending "safe." If bankruptcy insurance were available to stop you from going bankrupt, it still would not be able to prevent the emotional and social consequences of financial irresponsibility, and it certainly could never guarantee financial success.

The definition of saving is going without something now in order to have something better later on. Those who do it, economically or sexually, come out ahead (and are happier) than those who don't.

You may say any of the following: "But it's hard." "It sometimes goes against my basic physical instincts and urges." "It's unrealistic." "It won't work." "No one else is doing it." "It denies me what I need."

The first two statements are right. But so what? That's life. Almost everything of real value is hard, and the definition of maturity and discipline is controlling and channeling our instincts and urges. It is hard to earn, save, and be wise with money, just as it's hard to save and be wise with sex. Urges to spend are the reason it's hard.

The last four quotes are wrong. They are the very deceptions we have to watch out for and protect ourselves from. It's not unrealistic to save sex or to save money. Millions of people do it, and it does work. The final quote is the most accepted and the most dangerous of all, economically and sexually. Confusing our wants with our needs lies at the heart of so many bad decisions. We may think we need a newer car or a bigger house that we can't afford. "Needing it" seems so much more legitimate and acceptable than the more honest "wanting it." People do not have a genital need for casual or early sex. It is not an urge akin to eating or sleeping. We don't die if we don't do it. It is a want. It can be controlled, and it can be saved.

The economic and sexual ramifications of saving and spending are remarkably similar, with one huge difference: When you spend your money early and irresponsibly, the problem is simply that it's gone and you won't have it when you need it. When you spend your virtue early and irresponsibly, it is gone, too, and you won't have it when you need it (to add to the commitment and romantic exclusivity of a long-term relationship). But with sex that is not the only penalty. When you spend your virtue, it's not only what you won't have, it is also what you might have. One out of six sexually active teens gets a sexually transmitted disease. So to complete the analogy: In addition to spending all your money, you would be placing a cartridge in a six-shooter, spinning the cylinder, putting it to your head, and pulling the trigger.

DISCUSSION

Question: What does the article contend is the best protection against the physical, emotional, and mental dangers of sex?

Answer: To *save* it for a mature, committed, long-term relationship.

Question: In the author's view, what is the trouble with traditional "safe sex" or condoms?

Answer: They're not dependable and don't always work. Their goal is to avoid something bad, not to achieve something good. They don't protect people emotionally or mentally. They are a short-term rather than a long-term "solution."

Question: What is the basic definition of "saving"?

Answer: Going without something now in order to have something better later on.

Question: What is the similarity between "spending" sex rather than saving it and spending money rather than saving it?

Answer: It's gone—you won't have it when you need it—and you'll have less commitment and "romantic exclusivity" to give.

Question: What is the difference, the additional penalty, for spending sex that doesn't apply to spending money?

Answer: The one-in-six chance of getting a sexually transmitted disease.

Question: In what ways do you think that to "save sex" is better than "safe sex"? How relevant is this article to you personally?

Reading #7: Degrees of Abstinence

The problem with the word "abstinence" is that it's too broad. Does it mean waiting until you're sixteen to have sex? Does it mean waiting until you're married? Does it mean waiting until you're sure you're in love? The point is that there are different degrees of abstinence.

Let's refer to abstinence that means waiting until somewhat mature and somewhat committed as *degree one.* Let's refer to abstinence that means waiting until engaged as *degree two.* And let's refer to abstinence that means waiting until marriage as *degree three.*

If you choose to aim for degree one, you might expect a much easier time than if you aim for degrees two and three. After all, degree one is the accepted standard or ideal of most high school and college students, and it's fairly natural for kids to believe that anything else than this is irresponsible, exploitive, dangerous, even "slutty" behavior. If you choose degree one as your goal, you'll also have a lot of social and psychological experts on your side, commending you for a "realistic," "practical," "moderate" approach to the whole issue. It's a degree you can aim at that, while quite protective and conservative, is nonetheless not prudish or puritanical or ultra-ring-wing. It appeals to the high school and college notion of balance: "Don't be a slut but don't be a prude, either. Don't sleep around, but do have 'real' involvement with someone you really care about."

So degree one sounds pretty good, doesn't it? It's approachable, practical, possible.

Oh, how easily we are attracted to what sounds easy and acceptable. But think about it for a minute. Think clearly and critically about this compromised or partial abstinence, this one-partner-at-a-time "serial monogamy." Of course it is better to wait for some commitment than for none at all. But short of a true long-term commitment such as engagement or marriage, how do we define what commitment really is? The whole idea of commitment becomes shallow if it has no definition. "Well, I'm committed for quite a while, I think. I mean I like him, and I'm not going out with anyone else right now. We feel good about each other. We don't want to be with someone else tomorrow night. We're an item. So, yes, we're committed."

Probe that reasoning a little by asking how long commitment is. "Well, until it doesn't feel right anymore. Until we're not good for each other. Maybe until one of us graduates . . . or meets someone else . . . or whatever."

The problem is that these short-term, conditional commitments feel good, even feel right, but they are often nothing more than elongated, stretched-out one-night stands, and they almost always end with some pain. Young people say, "Oh, I'm sure when we break up we'll still be friends!" But don't count on it. Whatever the pain and guilt and regret of a one-night stand, it is multiplied in a multi-night stand. To say,

"We'll be together until it doesn't work for us anymore, and then we'll move on," is like saying, "We'll get married for a while and then get divorced when it doesn't work anymore."

Little one-month or six-month "commitments" are like little short-term marriages with built-in divorces. And despite what anyone says or hopes or tries to believe, divorce by any name is painful. The other problem is that one or more "minor commitments" dilute one's emotional and spiritual ability to make a "major commitment." The short term undercuts the long term. The "short time" undercuts the "lifetime."

Part of the justification for degree one abstinence is absolutely true. It is easier to aim at the bigger target, but it is better—harder and better—to aim at degree two. Engagement is an agreement to make a lifetime commitment, and abstinence until that point helps you avoid the whole serial monogamy syndrome that can be so painful.

If you're in agreement with the desirability of degree two abstinence, why not go all the way and aim for degree three? There is great surface appeal in the "logic" of "engagement as a trial marriage." And the new traditional wisdom of high school or college campuses is that "you have to see if you're physically and emotionally compatible with each other before you get married." In other words, "Don't buy a pair of shoes until you've tried them on."

Yet statistics show the opposite. Couples who live together before marriage have a substantially higher chance of divorce than couples who do not live together prior to marriage. The simple reality is that waiting for sex and cohabitation until marriage strengthens the marriage commitment, deepens marital loyalty, and increases the chance of a lasting marriage.

Based on this fact (and on your own inner feelings about what is best), wouldn't you agree that if it's best to wait until you're engaged, it's even better to wait until you're married?

If it seems like a "stretch of the realistic," then take it a step at a time:

Step One: Develop a positive, beautiful image and concept of sex as the most beautiful, awesome thing in the world.

Step Two: Conclude that it's too good to squander, too special to use with anyone but your most loved one.

Step Three: Understand the folly of too-early sex and the advantage of "saving," thus putting yourself at least in the prevailing attitude of degree one abstinence.

Step Four: As you get older, extend the same thinking and the same reasoning (the rewards, the delayed gratification, and even the statistics), and step up to degrees two and three.

DISCUSSION

Question: Which degree of abstinence does the article recommend?

Answer: Degree three.

Question: Why?

Answer: It's harder, but it's more logical and more beneficial.

Question: Which is the easiest degree of abstinence to pursue?

Answer: Degree one.

Question: Why?

Answer: It's a socially acceptable goal on high school and college campuses, and it's thought of as "realistic." Plus, it can be modified and rationalized so you can essentially reach it no matter what you do.

Question: Why isn't degree two a good compromise?

Answer: Because statistics show that people who cohabit between engagement and marriage increase their chances of divorce.

Question: What is serial monogamy, and what is the problem with it?

Answer: Serial monogamy is having one partner at a time and moving from one short-term monogamous relationship to another. The problem is that it's like a little series of short-term marriages and divorces, with lots of emotional pain.

Question: Does the author suggest that a person has to commit completely to degree three from the start?

Answer: No. The suggestion is that a person can start with degree one (in high school) and then extend the commitment to degrees two and three.

Question: What are your personal opinions about this essay and its implications for you?

Reading #8: Consequences of Casual Sex (from a Political and a Religious Perspective)

A POLITICAL PERSPECTIVE

America is plagued by a myriad of social problems, yet a strong case can be made that sex-related problems, encompassing everything from teen pregnancy to extramarital "cheating" and family breakup, are the most serious of all and have the most far-reaching ramifications.

One way to rank social problems is on a simple matrix that lists five criteria: (1) their economic costs, (2) their noneconomic costs, (3) the number and percentage of people directly involved, (4) the number and percentage of people directly affected, and (5) the links to other major social problems. On this matrix, sex-related social problems win the "severity contest" hands down. (See if you agree and, if you wish, fill in your opinion of the relative rankings of the other social problems listed.)

RANKING MATRIX OF SOCIAL PROBLEMS

	SEX-RELATED PROBLEMS	SUB-STANCE ABUSE	CRIME AND VIO-LENCE	POVERTY, HOMELESS-NESS	MISCEL-LANEOUS
1. Level of economic cost	1				
2. Level of noneconomic cost	1				
3. Number and percentage of people directly involved in the problem	1				
4. Number and percentage of people directly affected by the problem	1				
5. Cause and effect links to other social problems	1				

NOTE: Adult extramarital sex and "too-early" sex do not need to be separated in this matrix. Indeed, they need to be combined because they are statistically and causally linked. Each leads to and indeed *causes* the other.

NOTES ON CHART:

Line 1: No other social problem, not even crime or poverty, is as economically devastating. The direct and indirect costs of teen pregnancy and related child welfare, health, and judicial costs are truly staggering. And the attitude of instant gratification fostered by irresponsible sex has an economic counterpart: the materialism and credit abuse that block savings and investment, and weaken our economy.

Line 2: The noneconomic costs (which, by the way, often

result in or precipitate additional financial drains) are simply too great to measure. And when the most basic institution (family) breaks down, it forces the expensive growth of larger institutions (government) to try to correct the very problems that stronger families could have prevented.

Line 3: Far higher percentages of kids are involved in high-risk, too-early sex than in crime or in poverty or even in substance abuse. The same polls that show 20 percent of high school students use drugs show 60 percent of high school students are at risk through being sexually active. And a higher percentage of married people have engaged in extramarital affairs or incidents than have used drugs during their marriages.

Line 4: Whether directly involved or not, everyone is directly affected. Casual, experimental, recreational, or exploitative sex is essentially a family problem, and we are all part of families.

Line 5: Cause and effect between related social problems is always arguable, and there are those who say poverty brings about irresponsible, promiscuous sex. But it is more logical to argue the other direction. Casual sex in all its forms lowers the chance for survival of functional families, which are the best defense against poverty. And too-early sex is clearly linked with substance abuse, with the school dropout rate, with severe health risk, and with a host of other serious social problems.

A RELIGIOUS PERSPECTIVE

Many religions and their respective scripture suggest that the "sexual sins" of adultery and fornication are second only to murder in their seriousness. (And please note that if more of us were scripturally literate, there would be little need to create new words for dangerous, destructive, irresponsible forms of sex. Casual or irresponsible sex in the Bible has two simple and direct names: adultery and fornication.) Some theologians suggest four reasons that sexual sin ranks so high on the graveness scale:

1. It tampers with and trivializes life, especially the beginning of life, which (like the ending of life) is God's domain.
2. God tells us that our bodies are the temples of our spirits. As such, they should be respected and refined, not made coarse or crass by irresponsible out-of-marriage sex.
3. It destroys families, striking at the very core of the trust, commitment, and bond that most religions seek to strengthen and preserve.
4. Perhaps more than any other violation, the breaking of this commandment (as Christian and Jewish theology would call it) leads to and precipitates the breaking of other commandments. "Cheating" almost always involves lying, disrespect, and coveting, and to many theological minds has links to idolatry, "other gods," the stealing of virtue, and to what some perceive as terminating the life of unborn children. In other words, violation of one of the ten commandments leads directly to the breaking of at least seven others.

Many priests, rabbis, ministers, and other religious leaders (with much agreement from their spiritual communities) speak in terms of "the wages of sin" and the consequences that result from violating the different commandments or natural laws. This theory is rather simple and carries a certain "ring of truth" that makes it hard to refute. It says, in essence:

> *In some ways we are a far more moral people than earlier generations. Our "character" has improved in many ways in this country during the last fifty years. We are clearly more tolerant as a society, less prejudiced, and more truly believing in racial, gender, and virtually every other form of equality. We are more honest in many ways, due in part to the institutions that monitor us, including the media. We are more health conscious, more environ-*

mentally concerned, and probably more peace-loving. The one "value category" or aspect of character where we have experienced substantial spiritual and moral decline is in our sexual attitudes and activity.

The "wages" or consequences of sin, which are not vindictive punishments by God but simply the operation of eternal, natural law, are always particular and specific to the type and nature of the sin. In periods of prejudice, intolerance, and belief in the superiority of some humans over others, we received the "wages" of civil unrest and racial and other forms of prejudice, which led to violence and destruction. The wages of environmental and physical indifference and indulgence are the destruction and loss of beauty, health, and so on.

In our time, the escalation of sexual sin produces its own set of specific wages or consequences—the epidemic of AIDS and other STDs; the emotional loneliness of estranged, abandoned, or abused spouses, children, and elderly; the desensitization of relationships; and the destruction of families.

Those who believe in immortality are less likely to participate in immorality. If we believe we are ultimately held accountable for our actions, we are likely to be more cautious about what those actions are, as well as more aware of how they affect others.

DISCUSSION

Question: What are the essay's five criteria for ranking America's most serious social problems? Do you think these are the right criteria?

Answer: Economic cost, noneconomic cost, percentage of people involved, percentage of people affected, and responsibility for other social problems.

Question: Do you agree that sex-related problems should be ranked first in all five categories?

Question: How does the author justify his contention that sex-related problems are more serious than poverty or violence?

Answer: A higher percentage of people are involved and affected; the high costs; more likely to "spin off" and cause or precipitate other social problems; most destructive of all to families.

Question: Beyond damaging families and leading to other societal problems, what additional reasons from a religious perspective are offered as to why casual sex is such a serious problem?

Answer: It tampers with life, which is God's domain, and it disrespects our bodies, which are the temples of our spirits.

Question: In what ways does the author think we may be more moral today than earlier American generations? In what ways less?

Answer: We are more tolerant, honest, health conscious, and committed to equality. We are less sexually disciplined and responsible.

Question: What are the similarities between the political perspective and the religious perspective?

Answer: Both are attempts to gauge the seriousness of sexual problems. Both discuss the cause and effect relationship between casual sex and other societal problems. Both use consequences as the basis for their arguments.

Question: What is your opinion of this essay? In what ways is it relevant to you?

Reading #9: Four Perspective Poems About Sex

A NOTE, A MELODY, OR A SYMPHONY

Perhaps
music is the metaphor

for emotionally grasping
the profound differences between
the temporary instant gratification of casual sex,
the improvement of some commitment,
and the completeness of strong marriage.

Casual sex is a single note,
ringing perhaps,
maybe a momentary strong clear note
but alone, unconnected,
without context or cadence.
Repeated, it can be first redundant,
then boring, then monotonous,
then tedious, finally even torturous.

Committed sex is a melody,
a line of simple, pleasing music
linked and emotionally legible,
past and future tied,
somewhat secure but lacking sustained sacrificing passion,
without construction or compelling complexity,
thus wearing thin,
growing tiresome,
wanting change,
needing variety,
circling back on itself,
expecting expansion or completion . . . or to move on.

Consummate sex is a symphony,
harmonies deep and rich and subtle,
intricate, intimate instrumentation.
A blending of tenderness, power, and dissonance.
It soars and subsides, stirs and softens.
You could listen all your life
and never hear it all.

DISCUSSION

Question: What is the meaning of "tedious" and "tor-turous" with regard to a single musical note or to casual sex?

Question: What are the similar pros and cons of a single line of melody and a short-term sexual commitment?

Question: What differentiates a symphony from a simple melody? Do you think the comparison works for the consummate sex of a loyal marriage?

Question: What do you think of the poem's overall metaphor? Are the three levels of sex it portrays as different as the three levels of music?

THE REAL REASON IS FAMILY

Such unanimity in theory, in precept, in priority . . .
What do we want most?
What do we value most?
What matters most?
We all say . . . *family.*
We want career success or wealth or power.
We want friends and experience.
We value all these things.
But when pressed . . .
What matters most? *Most* say family.
Is it a wish or a goal?
Something we hope for or
Something we work for?

If a goal, what is the plan?
Since divorce is the family's most direct destroyer and
Since the two strongest statistical predictors of divorce are
Extramarital sex (infidelity after marriage) and
Premarital sex (promiscuity or cohabitation before marriage),
One essential plan element might be found
    in two old-fashioned words:
Fidelity and chastity.

Too simple, too basic?
Or is this the profound simplicity
    that lies beyond complexity?

Is this the master stroke?
Could the simple saving of sex be the symbol
Of the oneness, the loyalty, and the commitment
That keeps a family together?
Gets a marriage through the tough times?
Makes the home a safe haven?

Not a panacea, not a guarantee,
But saving sex puts statistics on your side,
Makes a simple, powerful, beyond-words statement
About your commitment and your love.

Fast-forward forty years:
View two virtual videos—you
With and without family.
See the faithfulness in the former,
Surrounded by support; caring and receiving care.
See the loneliness in the latter,
Induced by indiscretion—the heart cut out.

Something in us knows these long-term alternatives,
Craves one, fears the other.
Prompts us to prioritize family.
But the prompting must turn into a plan,
And one element in that plan
Is the physical practice, the emotional equilibrium,
    and the spiritual symbol
Of saving sex.

DISCUSSION

Question: What does the poem suggest is the most universal priority? most important goal? biggest threat to the priority and goal? cause or precipitation of that threat? way to combat that cause?

Question: Do you agree with this sequence?

Question: How does the fast-forwarding forty years enhance the point of the poem?

DESIGN OF A DARK FORCE

Imagine
that there was some sinister force
(intelligent, cunning, subtle, and strong)
trying to wreak havoc in our world
and to bring about widespread personal unhappiness.

Imagine that, in this end pursuit,
this dark force came up with subobjectives
or means to its disruptive ends:
To destroy our personal security
(make everyone feel isolated and "unlinked")
To break us economically
(introduce a financial collapse that devastates society)
To rob us of love
(short-circuit our ability to feel deep joy)
To create a group of human predators
(who feed their appetites on the weak and the young).

Complicated plan?
Multifaceted?
Or could one thing do it all?
Take sex, the life force, the love force,
and turn it
from consummation
to recreation.
That
will do it all.

DISCUSSION

Question: What do you think is the poet's main point?

Question: How do you think recreational or casual sex

destroys personal security? breaks us economically? robs us of love? creates human predators?

Question: What feelings or emotions does the poem convey to you?

DELAYED GRATIFICATION

"How much does the car cost?"
"$399 a month."
"No, I mean what is the actual cost?"
"The what?'
"The total price of the car!"
"I don't know. It costs me $399 a month, but I got a $1,000 cash rebate, so it doesn't cost me anything for the first three months."

Rebates.
Credit cards.
Minimum payments.
Lease to own.
No payments until next year.
Get it now.
A world of instant gratification
that saddles with debt,
undermines freedom.
Like a gluttonous king
we consume without counting the cost.
Everything is within reach—we grow fat.
We are without the tone and temper of
working, watching, waiting.

"Waiting":
a lost word, a lost joy.
In waiting was the long-held joy of anticipation,
a lean, hard discipline,
and the recalled joyful after-memory of the struggle.

In economic appetites,
instant gratification leads to debt, insolvency, bondage.
In physical appetites,
instant gratification causes obesity, debauchery;
In emotional appetites,
instant gratification promotes a casual, callous ingratitude.
In sexual appetites,
instant gratification brings deceit, disease, and despair.

But always . . . we are robbed most not by what they bring
but by what they take away.

DISCUSSION

Question: Does the poem portray "waiting" more as a responsibility or a joy?

Question: Why do you think the poem uses money and economics to make its point?

Question: Do you agree with the general sentiment of the poem?

Question: What is the meaning of the poem's last two lines?

A CONVERSATION WITH PARENTS WHO GAVE UP FOR THE WRONG REASONS

Old college friends, out of touch for twenty years. We've never met their children. A school reunion. We're catching up now. The subject turns to their worries over their kids.

"How things have changed," they lament. "Remember, we couldn't even have 'the opposite sex' in our dorm rooms. Now our daughters have boyfriends sleeping with them in their

rooms at home—in *our* house. Different nights, different partners."

"You're kidding," we say. (Be careful, don't offend.) "In
your home? Do you approve of that?"

"Well, no, we don't . . . not really? But how can you fight
it? It happens everywhere! We just decided we didn't want to
force them into a seedy hotel or the backseat of a car."

"Do your daughters confuse 'allowing it' with 'approval'?"

"No, they know how we feel . . . I think. We just gave up
and looked the other way. It wasn't worth destroying our relationship."

Troublesome, this thinking, this "logic." Would you let
your children lie and cheat and steal in your home so they
wouldn't have to go outside to do it? But it's even more troublesome because these parents gave up for the wrong reasons—on the false premise that everyone does it, that it's
hopelessly old-fashioned not to, that they can never influence
their children as profoundly as the media or the peer group,
that concepts such as abstinence and delayed gratification
could never appeal to a young person today, that parents who
live by and try to teach their own convictions would repel and
alienate children, destroying their relationship with them.

Not so! Not so! Not so! Everyone doesn't do it! And it's
new-fashioned not to. Parents can influence their children
most. True concepts and true convictions have deep and reso-
nant appeal, especially to our own children!

Other parents give up for different wrong reasons. "I can't
teach abstinence because I didn't live it. I'd be a hypocrite
to teach my kids something I didn't do." Hypocrite? Are you
restricted from teaching honesty because you once lied? Isn't
parenting about progress? About children learning from our
experience? Aren't some of the most valuable things we teach
our children those that we've learned through the kind of experience we hope they won't repeat?

The fact is that a great many parents—perhaps most—
want their kids to *wait*—some because of physical safety, some

for emotional protection, some for religious conviction, some for the simple principle of delayed gratification, some because they believe that something as "old-fashioned" as chastity is part of commitment and the precursor to the fidelity that could strengthen and save their child's marriage, the grand-children's happiness, and their long-term extended family stability.

Whatever the reason or reasons, most parents want their kids to wait, wish their kids would wait, wonder if they could wait. Wishing, wondering, and waiting are wistful words. Why not *do* more. Why not do everything possible to help this waiting to happen or to help it change if it hasn't been happening?

Notes

1. "Adolescent Sexual Involvement" by Stephen J. and Shelagh K. Genuis in *The Lancet* 345 (Jan. 28, 1995): 240, and 344, no. 8927 (Oct. 1, 1994): 899.
2. "Abstinence or Else!" by Jeff Stryker in *The Nation* 264, no. 23 (June 16, 1997): 19, and *Current Health* 20, no. 12 (Oct. 2, 1993): 1.
3. "The Failure of Sex Education" by Barbara Dafoe Whitehead in *Atlantic Monthly* 274 (October 1994): 55.
4. "Beyond the Birds and the Bees" by Liana R. Clark in *Patient Care* 32, no. 7 (Apr. 15, 1997): 102.
5. *The Nation* 264, no. 23 (June 16, 1997): 19, and *Current Health* 20, no. 12 (Oct. 1, 1993): 1.
6. *Ibid.*
7. "None, Not Safer, Is the Real Answer" in *Insight on the News* 10, no. 19 (May 9, 1994): 25.
8. "Beyond the Birds and the Bees" by Liana R. Clark in *Patient Care* 31, no. 7 (Apr. 15, 1997): 102.
9. "Social Costs of Teenage Sexuality" in *Society* 30, no. 6 (Sept./Oct. 1993): 3.
10. "Sex and Responsibility" by Jan Parrington in *Current Health* 22, no. 1 (Sept. 1995): 1.
11. *Ibid.*, p. 2.
12. "Learning to Say No" by John Leo in *U.S. News & World Report* 116, no. 24 (June 20, 1994): 24.
13. *American Journal of Public Health* 86 (1996): 565–68.
14. "Was It Good for Us?" by David Whitman in *U.S. News & World Report* 122, no. 19 (May 1997): 56.

15. *Ibid.*
16. "Centered on Families" by Dr. Jeffery Larsen and Dr. Bernard Poduska in *Brigham Young University Report,* Summer 1997.
17. "Good Sex Comes to Those Who Wait" by W. R. Mattox in *Family Policy* 6, no. 6 (1984): 1.
18. *U.S. News & World Report* 122, no. 19 (May 19, 1997): 56.
19. *Ibid.,* p. 57.
20. *Ibid.*
21. *Ibid.*
22. *Ibid.*
23. T. B. Heaton, *Family Trends,* 1997. Brigham Young University.
24. *U.S. News & World Report* 122, no. 19 (May 19, 1997): 56.
25. *Ibid.*
26. *The 1996 Kaiser Foundation Survey on Teens and Sex.* Kaiser Family Foundation, Reuters, Dec. 12, 1996.

Afterword

Why Parents and Families Are the Answer

We should end where we started, with ourselves as parents, with our stewardship and responsibility, with the simple (and joyful—because we wouldn't want it any other way) realization that it's largely up to us.

Some abdicators say, "We can't set goals for our children. They have to set them for themselves." Rather than argue, let's just modify. Our goal must be to teach them, help them, motivate them, and protect them long enough to allow them to set the right goals for themselves.

Parents who look for solutions become the solution.

Regaining Power

One of the reasons that much of this book comes in the form of dialogues and discussions is that it is the most effective way we know to get information and feelings across to children. The other reason is that dialogue and discussion formats are user-friendly enough to *re-empower* parents. When your children were small, you felt no hesitation in telling them what you thought, what you felt, what they should and shouldn't do, and what was best for them. Often, as children get older, parents get timid—unfortunately and ironically at just about the time that kids need specific guidance, direction, and limits.

The discussions and your commitment to be the major influence in your child's life can help you regain your rightful position (and your confidence) as a parent.

The initial response of some parents to some of the dialogues is that they are leading or manipulative, that they try to steer kids toward conclusions about abstinence and restraint. Actually, the discussions respect children and give them credit for being able to think about things logically and answer questions thoughtfully. And where they do attempt to steer and influence, there should be no apology. As parents, our job and our stewardship is to guide, to lead, and to influence for good. The powerful, multi-billion-dollar industries of advertising and media are holding nothing back in their efforts to influence and manipulate our children. Their constant push for instant gratification and indulgence requires every countereffort and preemptive strike that we can provide.

Preventive Medicine

No conscientious and concerned parent would neglect to have their children vaccinated or given medical attention that protects their health. And we all recognize that preventive medicine is preferable to treatment after illness has begun.

Taking the time and making the effort to teach sexual restraint and responsibility is an emotional as well as a physical "vaccination." With a smallpox vaccination, a weakened or mock form of the disease is introduced into the body so that the child develops antibodies or resistance. In a similar fashion, the dialogues and role-plays that parents have with young children introduce the kinds of pressure and influence they will face, but in a safe and controlled "practice" setting, with the parent there to help. The child develops mental and emotional antibodies of resistance and the patterns of clear thought that will get him or her to prevail against the afflictions he or she will face in the years ahead.

Intimate Subjects, Intimate Settings

One of the most appealing metaphorical descriptions of a good home is a "safe harbor from the storm." In our children's lives, home should be not only a safe place but a place where they can learn safety, where they can put on the armor that protects them when they are outside the home.

Just as we don't want the world to hurt our children, we don't want it to jar them or disillusion them or deceive them or catch them off guard. Good discussions are like vicarious experiences. Some of the principles of safety and restraint and even good decision-making can be learned without entering the school of hard knocks because we can transfer to our children much of our experience and judgment.

The more intimate the subject, the more important that it be taught in an intimate setting. Schools, peers, and the rest of the world will teach our children a lot about sex, but the core of what they know and, most important, what they *feel* about sex should be learned in the setting where we hope consummate sex will someday occur: in the home, in their own family.

Balancing Strictness and Trust

Remember the study mentioned earlier that indicated too-strict parents are second only to completely lax parents in losing their kids to substance abuse, sexual promiscuity, and other forms of rebellion? Parents who learn to balance firmness and flexibility stand the best chance, and their children stand the best chance, in today's world.

The key to this balance is learning to blend *rules* and *reasoning* so that children view the behavior patterns as logical and capable of producing good results and consequences. Once rules are set via logical discussions and cause-and-effect reasoning, you are in a position to be flexible and make "trust-showing" exceptions as circumstances suggest. For example, if you fifteen-year-old has a weekend curfew of midnight and calls at 11:45 on a Saturday night to say that the video he and his friends are watching has twenty or thirty minutes to go and he can get a ride and be home before 12:30, you are well advised to say, "Thanks for calling so I wouldn't worry, son. That will be fine." (You might add a question like "Who is the ride with?" or a statement like "Let's not make a habit of this," but what you convey is trust and confidence and appreciation that he takes the curfew seriously. Besides, he has a ride in half an hour; you won't have to get dressed and go out to get him!)

Another example: Let's say you've discussed and thoroughly explained and set a rule of no one-on-one dating before age sixteen. (And this *is* a reasonable and appropriate rule.) Your fifteen-year-old freshman who turns sixteen in two months is dying to go to the high school Christmas dance. Instead of an arbitrary, rigid interpretation of the rule, compromise with a "group date" with several other couples, driven to and from the dance by parents.

Parents often fail to give their children the security and demonstration of love and concern that rules and limits provide. This common failure was poignantly illustrated in the movie *The Ice Storm* (which brilliantly depicts the immense damage and danger of the 1970s sexual revolution) when a father finally broaches the subject of sex to his adolescent daughter. The daughter is looking for and hoping for direction, guidance, and limits, but all the father says is "Don't get pregnant."

Strictness and trust, like responsibility and respect, are complementary, not contrary!

Reality Versus Theory: Teaching by Who We Are

We know we've already said it, but it bears saying again: Don't fail to teach your kids what you believe is best for them and safest for them because you didn't happen to do the same thing when you were younger. Remember that this is not about you or about the past. It is about your kids, about what is happening now and what will (and should) happen in the future. A good parent wants his child to benefit from something he didn't do perfectly just as much as from something he did.

Besides, times have changed, and you may have changed, too—more than you may realize. If you had more sex in your youth than you hope your children will have and yet are part of the 80 percent of married people who have never had an extramarital affair, then you are living what you are teaching.

In any case, keep the goal in front of you: to protect your child and to maximize his or her chances for a happy life with lasting relationships.

Whatever you are that is in harmony with what you want and hope for your child, emphasize it, show it, talk about it. If you are married and love your spouse, and feel loyal and committed to him or her, *tell* your child. Let your child see your affection. Talk about how special it is to love each other and be loyal and faithful to each other.

The whole point of basing all discussions on the "beautiful

and awesome" theme, and of establishing happiness and joy rather than fear as the prime reasons for being both knowledgeable and wise about sex, is that positive reasons are more motivational and more lasting than negative ones. If joy is the message and the motive, kids are given something to work for rather than something to avoid. Strive to be a *model* for what you teach. If you are a two-parent family, you should live by and exemplify the "beautiful and awesome" theme. Let your kids see in you what they want to strive for in their own marriage.

There are two obvious benefits in doing this: First, your kids are happier and have more to strive for. Second, you are happier because you are striving!

LINDA'S SUMMARY

Let me begin by saying how sad I think it is that so many children in our society are being raised by institutions. Institutions used to be schools, churches, hospitals, and residences for the mentally ill, the handicapped, the aged, the incorrigible, and the orphaned. Today we have to include in our list of institutions movies, television, magazines, tabloids, computer games, the Internet, Super Nintendo, and the full gamut of child care facilities. A shocking number of children today get their value system from the slick look and gaunt eyes of MTV images, learn responsibility from the electronic beeps of Giga Pets and Nano Babies, and are supervised, counseled, and nurtured by per-hour child care staff.

"What's a parent to do?" we say as we throw up our hands in despair. "The media is in control! Work leaves me no time for my kids." Many parents have essentially given up. For whatever reason—their own bad experiences in childhood, their loss of sensibility or sensitivity, alcoholism, drug dependency, or just plain disinterest in being a parent—many parents will never teach their children the principles or values that could enrich their lives. Because of this, we should all be grateful for the safety nets provided by churches and religious education, youth organizations, boys' and girls' clubs, caring teachers, and healthy sex education in the schools. But the fact remains: There is no place like home to teach and nurture, to love and educate your children about life and love.

One of my favorite possessions is a beautiful bronze sculpture of a baby, a palm-size handful of metal that personifies the joy and innocence of a newborn child, still in the fetal position, fresh from God. We believe that every infant's mind is like a seedling, ready to grow according to how well you care for it. The best care includes emotional communication, the unconditional, natural love that only a parent can give. Feed your children with things you love, water their interest by exposing them to what you want them to know, fertilize them by teaching them correct principles so they can make good decisions for themselves, and expose them to the sunlight of praise so they will gain confidence. And talk to them about love—in its finest sense.

A letter from the daughter who is the proud mother of our first grandson says: "I'm surprised that this baby's face is not entirely worn away with kisses!" Infants are so tender and easy to love. Things get harder as we tramp through the terrible twos and begin to see things we don't approve of in our child's behavior. If we don't continue to talk and consciously make time to discuss feelings, our seedlings will grow wild and sometimes out of control.

"But I don't communicate very well because my parents didn't communicate very well!" and "My child just doesn't tell me how she feels!" are responses we often hear from exasperated parents. They tell us they are concerned about what their child is thinking or feeling. They are frustrated because they don't know how to communicate with their child. We hope the dialogues in this book will assist them. I didn't start out as a very good communicator, either. (And Richard always communicates more than I want him to! Just kidding.) The bottom line here is: *Just do it!* Force yourself, entice yourself, reward yourself—do whatever it takes to let your child know that you love him enough to teach him sound principles, to let him know what you think, feel, and believe about sex and how a healthy attitude about it will make a profound difference in his life.

At my church I am working with a group of thirty-three girls, ages twelve to eighteen. Last Sunday I handed ten of the oldest girls—sixteen and over—a questionnaire to fill out anonymously. Each girl sat in an isolated spot in a large room to ensure total privacy. The theme of the questionnaire was living in a world with destructive influences. There were questions about how they felt concerning the help they were receiving at church and at home to avoid bad influences and encouraging them to talk about drugs, alcohol, and sex. You could probably not find better families than those from which these girls came, and this made many of their responses very surprising. Seven out of ten said that while they felt the church was doing its part in helping them avoid negative or destructive influences, they seldom if ever talked about such matters with their parents. The majority said that they didn't think their parents really knew what their problems were, and because of that, they'd rather talk about them with a friend. Several wished their parents would ask them more about their feelings and problems, and would talk to them about solutions in a nonjudgmental way.

Talking to your child in your home about sex is the answer to more of society's problems than you can guess. If all of us parents would build our own fortress of love by building relationships of trust, openness, and love from the moment the newborn child is placed in our arms, there is no doubt that, individually and collectively, we could change the world!

RICHARD'S SUMMARY

I'm going to be a bit ethereal here for my last few words and hope it won't detract from the practical, workable, "real-world" tone we've tried to give this book. I want to tell you something of a personal fable based on some experiences Linda and I had when we were just starting our family. I hope it will convey the bigger picture of how talking to your children specifically about sex can help them (and you) in much broader ways.

The sun had set behind the Tetons, backlighting them against the darkening autumn sky. Linda and I were in Jackson Hole, Wyoming, just the two of us, for a short vacation—the first since our honeymoon, and it was the first time we'd been away for any length of time from our two baby daughters. It was supposed to be a little break from the demands of parenting. The problem was that after the first couple of days, we missed those two little girls like crazy and were having a hard time thinking about anything else.

We had kind of a mystical experience that night in the shadow of those mountains as night fell. It wasn't something we'd asked for—at least it didn't seem so at the time—and it isn't easy to explain. Some might call it an epiphany or an inspiration or some kind of vision. Whatever it was has had a profound effect on our lives and was, in a way, the genesis of this book.

We were sitting on a log rail fence, having driven out to a remote lookout spot for no other reason than to gaze at those awesome, jagged peaks and watch the colors change as the sun dropped behind and silhouetted them. We had been talking about our daughters, and though we weren't saying anything at the moment, I knew Linda was thinking about our two babies. And I was, too—about our love and hopes and dreams for them, and about the daunting challenge of parenting and how to succeed in this new role.

Time seemed to stretch out. The sky and the mountains went from twilight to dusk to dark very gradually, and our minds as well as our eyesight seemed exceptionally, unusually clear. It seemed that I could see individual fir trees impossibly far away on the Grand Teton. With mental clarity, there were suddenly two concepts that seemed illuminated, obvious, and undoubtable, two concepts that I recognized as the keys to our parenting and to the happiness of our children. They weren't concepts we had talked or thought about at any length, and they didn't seep gradually into my mind or result from discussion or study or brainstorming. They were just there—complete, clear, and so undeniably true that it seemed everyone must know them, that all parents who love their children must grasp that these are the two indispensable needs. I can't say whether the concepts came by way of some kind of inner voice or whether the thought or message had a clarity that didn't need words and simply existed as something I knew. As I tried to explain what I was feeling to Linda, the two concepts seemed clear beyond the words I was using to explain them. That is why it will be difficult to convey them here, because they are more than words. But if you, the reader, will try to put your mind somewhere near where our minds were that night—focused on your love for your children and your worries about raising them in today's world—then you may feel these two answers the way I did that night.

The first concept that came so powerfully to me was *communication*. It was almost as if I could see our daughters growing up, their lives unfolding from childhood to adolescence to adulthood with the powerful pull of peer group and of media, with the difficulty of decisions and the pain of disappointments and I saw clearly how every challenge was softened and how every bit of love was enhanced by our communication with them and theirs with us. Communication suddenly was a concept that meant trust, sharing, courage, and safety. And I saw that it was the antidote to rebellion, fear, alienation, and naive, dangerous mistakes. If we could just keep communication open with them as they grew up—if there were no secrets, no off-limit subjects, no generation gap, no big or lasting lies—we would, over time, succeed as parents.

We had thought about and talked about communication before, but this concept, this powerful need, was now so clear and complete. Open communication with our kids would save them. I saw that clearly. It made every other good parental goal possible. And without it everything was at risk, out of the sphere of our influence, and might not even be known by us until too late.

The other concept was a term I probably had never used before, yet in the perceptiveness of that night it seemed to counter all the negative forces we had been discussing about the world our children would grow up in—all the self-indulgence, the materialism, the desire to have everything and do everything and be everything now. The term used over and over in this book was new to me then. It was *delayed gratification*. I knew at that moment, with certainty, that if we could find a way to teach, to really convey to our children, both the wisdom and the joy of waiting, of saving, of restraint—in short, of delayed gratification—we would be protecting them from the most frequent causes of economic failure and personal unhappiness, and we would be giving them the formula for creating stable, balanced, and fulfilled lives.

Linda and I spent the last few days of our vacation talking about the two concepts and about how mysteriously and clearly they had come that night as the sun set and the moon rose.

The two "solutions" didn't falter or break down with discussion. They got stronger. We thought of friends who had problems with kids and realized that, in each case, better communication or better application of delayed gratification could have avoided or solved the problem. We began to believe what we still believe: *That any parent who does whatever it takes to keep communication open with kids and who works continually at teaching and exemplifying the principle of delayed gratification in all wants, desires, and appetites will succeed, and children of such a parent will survive and thrive physically, emotionally, and spiritually.*

There is a "part two" to this personal epiphany, and it is the part that links it directly to this book. Nearly ten years later, as our third child, Josh, approached the age of eight, I happened to be back in Jackson, on a fishing trip this time, floating along in a rubber boat on the Snake River. I was thinking about Josh and about the "age eight" discussion we would have with him the following week. As the river current pulled me along, I looked up at the sunlit Tetons and was taken back to the experience ten years earlier when looking up at the same mountains.

It came to me then—with the same suddenness and clarity—that by far the most significant thing we had done to implement the concepts of communication and delayed gratification with our two daughters was the series of discussions we'd had with them about sex. It was like the completion of an answer, the finishing of a message after ten years. I understood at that moment that with all the efforts we'd made since committing ourselves to those two concepts, nothing had furthered them, implemented them, activated them like our recent interchanges about growing up, about puberty, about sex and romantic love and marriage.

The intimacy of these subjects had allowed a warmer, more respectful, more sharing and trusting kind of communication with our daughters than any other subject at any other time. It had opened a channel of communication and emotional trust in which we felt a new confidence that we could and always would be able to communicate with our children about anything and everything. And this subject, as we thought about it, was more squarely and more dramatically about delayed gratification than anything else we had ever (or would ever) talk about. We realized that it had set a stage where other kinds of delayed gratification could be discussed.

Our discussions about sex were not the closing of a door on that subject but were the opening of other doors that allowed us to talk and teach principles of responsibility and restraint, of seeking and saving.

I said a little prayer that day as I swept along beneath the mountain splendor. It was a prayer of gratitude for the insights that had come to me there ten years before.

The simplicity and the validity of what came to me in the mountains on that one autumn evening and on that one autumn morning ten years later have really been the motivation for this book. Since then we've had our age eight discussions with Josh and then six more times, with six more children. Each time these discussions about sex have brought us emotionally and spiritually closer to the child. Each time the principles we talked about "took" and had a powerful influence on the sexual behavior and the emotional and physical safety of that child. Each time the discussion opened up and reinforced a level of trust and communication that has endured and has given us a clearer view of the delayed gratification principle. We've applied this principle to all sorts of topics and situations, and we believe it will literally save our kids.

The mountain led us to it. May this book be your mountain!

Finding a Support Group

As we've received feedback from parents who have listened to or read our ideas on teaching children about sex, one type of response really gives us pause and begs to be addressed at the end of this book. It goes like this: "It all sounds right to me. I think it's the best way to go. I want to teach almost everything in here to my kids, to convince them to practice sexual responsibility and restraint. But I just don't think I can do it—not by myself. I need a support group of some kind, not just to reinforce what I teach my kids, but to reinforce *me*."

In a way this type of response makes us feel guilty. We try to empower parents, to tell them they can do it, to tell them that lots of parents have done it and are doing it, even to tell them that *we've* done it. But then we pause. And when we're really honest with ourselves, we know we couldn't have done it on our own. No parent can. Parents can be the center, the mainstay, but they need support. In our case that support came mostly from our church, which teaches responsibility and restraint and, yes, *virtue.* The church reinforces and backs up our position, and it motivates us to do our best as parents.

So we cannot conclude without suggesting that you find something similar. Some of you already have it—a church, a parents' group, a values-oriented private school, a scout troop, something that reinforces the values you teach and keeps you motivated in teaching them. If you don't have something, find something, something bigger to be a part of.

A church with active teachings in these areas is best. As an additional alternative, we can offer you a parents' support organization that we founded twenty years ago called S.J.S. HOME-BASE. It is essentially a parents' co-op that has more than 100,000 members throughout the world, all of whom are trying to teach *values* and *joy* and *responsibility* to their children. Members receive newsletters, tapes, and workbooks, but most of all they receive the reinforcement, motivation, and identity that comes from being part of a group with shared goals and ideals. Call the HOMEBASE office at (801) 581-0112 for further information.

About the Authors

Linda and Richard Eyre live with their family in Washington, D.C.; Salt Lake City, Utah; and Jackson Hole, Wyoming. The mission statement of their nonprofit foundation **EYREALM** is "Popularize Parenting, Validate Values, and Bolster Balance." They are hard at work on their next book, *Turning the Hearts: Re•Value•ing the American Family.*